RING THE BELL

Whoever rings the bell the loudest, makes the most
money & leaves the greatest impact

JON MAJAK

Home Service Marketing & Mindset Expert

CONTENTS

ABOUT THE AUTHOR

 Jon Majak is a serial entrepreneur from South Florida. With over 25 years of business experience, Jon excels in mental toughness and marketing systems. He started from humble beginnings and built and sold several companies from the ground up including one of the busiest service companies in Florida.

After selling the company, he launched Mr. Pipeline, which helps service businesses scale to the highest level possible through results-driven digital marketing. He is also a Contributor to Forbes, Investor and Business Coach that is passionate about helping people leverage adversity into self-made millions. In his downtime, Jon enjoys spending time with family, traveling and advocating for mental health.

JonMajak.com

PROLOGUE

This book isn't for every business owner.

I also know that I probably shouldn't start off saying this, but it's true. This book is intended for the home service entrepreneur who wants to scale their business to the highest level possible by leveling up their mental toughness and being an absolute marketing machine.

It's for the entrepreneur who wants to make a difference and leave a lasting impact in this world. It's safe to say that if you are reading this book, you want to dominate your market and shine as bright as possible. If this is you, then you're going to enjoy this ride. Now let's get to work!

DEDICATION

Lauren: Thank you for being my angel on earth, my soulmate and my ride or die. Your strength and determination inspire me every day of my life. I pray that blessings rain down on you and your beautiful soul forever. Never stop being the light in people's lives. I love you more than you'll ever know.

Camden: May the wind always be at your back and the sun shine upon your face, beautiful boy. Don't ever forget that the words "I can't" are not in your vocabulary. You can do anything, and I mean anything, your heart desires. I love you.

Dad: You taught me that this game called business is only for the strong and resilient. I'll be forever grateful to you for your life & business wisdom. Keep inspiring us all!

Jonny D: My best man. My best friend. Thank you for being my constant and always believing in me no matter what. You make me feel a lot less alone in this crazy world. I love you, kid. I would never want to do any of this without you.

FOREWORD

Many people love jobs but hate job creators.

Isn't that fascinating?

Many despise the successful not because these high achievers have actually done something wrong but because they expose how small most people have played their own game of life.

It is easy to throw rocks from the sidelines, in the shadows.

It is effortless to blame others' achievements as the reason our own destiny has been sidelined.

Entrepreneurship is like jumping off a cliff and building a plane on the way down.

I can attest, from personal experience, the accuracy of this metaphor.

The extreme highs and lows are all a part of stepping into the unknown and walking the narrow road in pursuit of your dreams.

I have been bankrupt, broke, mocked and ridiculed.

I have been down and out and kicked by circumstance.

I have been laughed at and looked down upon.

What may look to be a string of bad luck is the very thing that built my capacity to change my life.

These so-called set-backs were actually a surprise gift that toughened me up and built my muscles.

After all, a muscle can only get stronger after it is ripped, torn and worked.

Getting punched by the school bully is only scary until you have taken a few good licks and then have the revelation that it doesn't hurt that bad after all.

Then, you start swinging back, and the bullies seem to vanish.

After all, bullies aren't looking for a fight; they are looking for a victim.

When you are gazing from the bottom of this journey, I want to encourage you to keep your eyes on the prize, not the obstacles.

Because, like the bully, those obstacles are not as scary as they initially seem, and their purpose is to test your resolve.

The average man will live his life never knowing the pain of failure or the pressure of real risk, the way a business owner does.

In fact, most people are happy to sit in the shadows and criticize the small few willing to imperfectly step into the arena of business.

From what I can tell, you, my friend, are not 'most people'.

The person who buys and reads a book like this is definitely different from the masses.

Another example is the man who worries he may not be a good father.

The truth is that he has much less to worry about than he thinks.

You see, bad fathers don't stress about such thoughts, just like most people don't dream about changing the world.

The fact that you are nervous and uncertain to embark on this business journey is evidence that you have what it takes in the first place, hunger.

In the Bible, it talks about how God's word is a lamp unto our feet.

It doesn't say that it is a 30-mile spotlight.

Have you ever thought about that?

A lamp only provides a few feet of illumination while you are traveling in darkness.

Building a successful business from the ground up, especially if it is your first time, is supposed to feel like this.

You can only find the answers when you are in motion and moving forward.

Fear acts as the natural filter that keeps most people broke, stuck and playing small.

One of the big secrets you will discover is that the obstacles aren't as scary as you think, and the rewards are far beyond money, although that is a particularly nice bonus.

Is it easy?

Certainly not, but it is worth it.

One of my favorite quotes is that 10 out of 10 people die.

Another good quote is that a wise man thinks of death often.

Why? Because everyone pays the same price for whatever they pursue on this Earth.

We all trade our life for our pursuits.

If you pursue nothing, it still costs you your life.

If you pursue greatness, the price remains the same.

Isn't it reasonable to make sure the journey you are embarking on will be worth it when then the final invoice called death comes knocking?

I think so.

Ringing the bell changes the world.

Ringing the bell changes you.

Ringing the bell is a gift to your customers, staff and Family.

When given the choice between safety and adventure, I'd choose adventure every single time.

Why?

Because it is not about reaching the destination, it is about who you become along the way.

Lean into your desire for more.

Don't apologize for being a change maker.

You will have the last laugh when the curtains close on your life, and you look back at the ripple effect your bell ringing has caused.

In closing, let's look at one of the most famous job recruitment ADs in history.

This was ran by Sir Earnest Shackleton in 1907 and was inviting men to join an expedition to the antarctic.

It read like this:

"Men wanted for hazardous journey. Low wages, bitter cold, long hours of complete darkness. Safe return doubtful. Honour and recognition in event of success."

It is said that this simple newspaper AD produced over 5,000 applicants!

Keep in mind this was the early 1900's, and people had to apply in person!

The question is, WHY? WHY was it such a success?

The answer is simple.

Men were created to pursue adventure and have an unshakable desire to trade their lives for something epic.

Unfortunately, society and schools have told us to sit quietly in the corner and mind our manners.

Remember this; you have two choices in this short life.

Option 1: Spend it creating someone else's dream.

Option 2: Spend it creating your own dream.

Happy bell ringing!

Sincerely,

Joshua Latimer

HonorAndFire.com

CHAPTER 1:
THE NARROW ROAD

E*ntrepreneurship is one incredible journey. Every venture you seek to conquer always starts out the same way, on the narrow road.*

It starts with an idea and then believing in yourself so much that you actually pursue that thought with every ounce of your being. Once the euphoria of launching a business fades away, you find yourself in your own mind quite often, pondering and trying to feed the good thoughts and swat down any self-doubt that may arise. You're on the dark, lonely narrow road, and it's filled with so much uncertainty. It's also somehow filled with such beauty.

One thing I know for sure is that entrepreneurship offers so much fulfillment, along with the greatest personal and professional growth plan, over anything else in the world. If you do it right, you even reap the true freedom it offers and the massive compensation plan that comes along with it. So make sure you bring some food, water, decent shoes, and a lantern - you're definitely going to need it.

As I start this book, I must give a shoutout to everyone who picked up a copy and commend you for wanting to build the life and business of your dreams, all while serving, giving back, and making a real impact in this world. My promise to you is simple and hopefully very easy to grasp. I promise to deliver real value to you.

This isn't one of those books built on vague and gray business ideas that hopefully you can make sense of. Each chapter following this will describe a part of the vision of what "Ring the Bell" actually means. I am intentionally starting each chapter by painting a vision of each milestone along the way to the top of the mountain.

I do this for two reasons. First, I am a big believer that once we can create a real vision in our minds, we are much more likely to resonate with the narrative. The second reason is that injecting some storytelling into a business book is unconventional, and that's what I'm all about.

Mark Cuban says it best: "Go where they ain't."

Additionally, the chapters will be filled with real-world business insight and gold nuggets that you can take to the bank. As you progress through this journey with me, we will stop and briefly rest. But this rest isn't to sit down and put our feet up. This rest is designed to be a weapon for you.

Isaac Newton said: "If I have seen further, it is by standing on the shoulders of giants." That's why in almost every chapter, I'll abruptly stop and inject an area called Campfire Chat with an Expert Climber. I've carefully selected eight contributor giants that have dedicated their valuable time to sharing massive insight; they over-deliver.

It's also worth mentioning that I might start sentences off wrong and do things, unlike a professional writer. That's because I believe in being imperfect and just executing and pouring my heart out. English scholars take it easy. Hopefully, the value I bring not only inspires you but allows your beautiful and analytical minds to look the other way.

If you are reading this right now, there's a high chance that you are walking the narrow road as we speak. So by now, you must be wondering- What does the narrow road look like? Well, it's different for everyone considering we all see life through a different lens. But one commonality that sticks out is the narrow road is dark, with little to no light in sight.

To take it further, perhaps it's a dark dirt road, and it's covered in thick overgrown trees, couldn't be muggier, and screams hopelessness. It's even safe to say that not many people even know you or that your courageous ideas exist at this point in the game. If this is the case, then smile, take a deep breath and know each step you take is leveling you up in some way. Well, if you are bold enough, of course. Even though it's pitch black out, your intuition told you to bring a lantern. That practical thinking not only strengthens your mindset but also simply allows you to put one foot in front of the other so you can see a few steps ahead of you. Even though you see and hear mysterious animals and creatures moving around beside you, you bring a knife and are willing to do whatever it takes to make it out alive. Even though your future is uncertain, you have moments where you smirk with confidence because you didn't realize how much your soul is set on fire when you follow your calling. The thrill of the unknown journey is real, and it's unlike anything you have ever felt.

Lastly, even though you can turn around at any moment and head back to the safe place where you started, you push forward, knowing you are discovering your purpose and you are making a choice to go get whatever your heart desires so much. No one is making you do it. How incredibly special is that?

The thing about the narrow road is that it gives zero fucks about you. It's actually pretty cool when you think about it. It doesn't coddle you or give you a snack when you do well. It's objective. It's real. It's raw. It crushes most, and the few fortunate ones who make it out alive are given the opportunity to see the next milestone. As Elon Musk said: "Being an entrepreneur is like eating glass and staring into the abyss of death."

In my life, there have been many times that I've never made it out of the narrow road alive. I had a great business idea in my head and, throughout the process, got wrapped up in the overgrown weeds plenty of times. You might even say I didn't have enough belief in the idea or just didn't straight up execute like the monster I needed to be. I mean it when I say that I'm so glad the road chewed me up and spit me out on some of those ideas.

On the other hand, though, well, that's a beautiful feeling. I can tell you from experience many times over that something amazing happens when you blaze a trail, walk the narrow road and make it out successfully. You are overcoming the odds, smashing down crippling fear, and somehow creating a path and roadmap for others. You are ripping out thorn-filled brushwood and making it through the mud to get to the ultimate destination.

"Being an entrepreneur is like eating glass and staring into the abyss of death."

Elon Musk

That means without knowing it, you're creating a path to help others follow suit. You're creating a way to lead people to the top, and that's the best way to go about it because, in my opinion, life is no fun when you do everything yourself. Life is remarkable when you bring others with you for the ride and see how wonderful it is to see them light up with joy. It's almost impossible to recognize it during the grind, but your pain and your struggle quite literally are helping other entrepreneurs, employees, friends, and family members in ways you would never imagine.

It's safe to say that you see this really clearly when you make it through the road. Let me recount a few examples of this. I'll never forget when my best friend got in major trouble when we were young. He got caught up in the wrong crowd, and let's just say he ended up selling some illegal stuff to get ahead in life. This wasn't like him at all, but needless to say, we were young, and it happened. During this moment in time, he got caught and served time in federal prison for years, and I helplessly watched his extremely bright future slip away from him.

At least that's what it felt like at the moment. When he was in prison, I showed up for him as much as I knew how to by writing letters, visiting him at three different federal prisons across the country, and sending him as much money as I could. Oftentimes, I would send him almost every dollar I had. Little did I know that God was rebuilding him behind those prison bars, and it's safe to say that alongside him, God was building me up as well.

My narrow road struggle was able to give him hope that when he came out, he could join my team and even work with me if he chose to. I sent him books on the business so he could study and grow as much as possible. When he was released, he joined my company, and in no time, both of us grinded our way into an almost eight-figure business. Imagine that!

Here's another one for you. Along my journey, I've had employees tell me that I literally saved their life. For example, I learned that a young man who was working for me fell on hard times in his past life. We never really spoke about it, but we both knew something had happened in the past. My thoughts on him were that he was such a good young man, and truthfully, I have never felt like I was in a position to judge him or anyone for that matter. I found out years later when he told me behind closed doors that he was grateful to share his life with me and that the work I provided for him kept him out of trouble, made him focus on sobriety, and offered a safe space for his mind, body, and soul. Talk about a good feeling!

Here's another example. I've had loyal friends sit with me at my office when I had no logo, no clients, or no clue what I was doing. Some would stop by just to check-in. Some would stop by to see how they could help me or simply drop by to have lunch and catch up. Nevertheless, the common theme was them showing up to support me and letting me know I had too many gifts to give the world and to not let them down. Whether they said it directly or implied it indirectly, that honor burned deep inside me.

Years later, those same friends reminded me of those humble times when I was genuinely stuck on the narrow road. When all I had was one dimly lit lantern that was kept burning by ambition. Now, many of them candidly tell me that it was in those moments when I started that I taught them that nothing was impossible if you truly want it bad enough. I'm so grateful for those kind words because I don't do what I do only for the money; of course, money is one of the key aspects, but what matters at my core is making a real difference and real impact on people's lives. The exact purpose of this book.

I'm sharing these personal moments not to boast one bit but rather to inspire you. Because if a kid who came from nothing, with no money and no experience, can make it through the narrow road, you can too.

If you are currently in the initial phase or facing a tough chapter in your business, I have some straightforward advice for you; as someone who has walked the path pretty much his entire life, keep pushing. As the great Abraham Lincoln once said: "I walked slowly, but I never walked backward." When you feel like turning around and starting over, keep going. When the ones you trust the most show you signs that they doubt you, keep on keeping on. Because when you finally make it to the end of the road, you can breathe easy again, and you will feel a sense of real accomplishment and pride knowing you achieved the impossible.

"Something amazing happens when you blaze a trail and walk the narrow road. You overcome the odds, smash down fear and somehow create a path and roadmap for others."

Jon Majak

According to the Small Business Administration, more than fifty percent of businesses fail within the first five years. When you make it through the narrow road, you've made it through the moments that you were statistically supposed to fail.

That's something no one can ever take away from you. If you have already made it through this phase, then don't just brush it off. If you're anything like me, you push real hard and don't stop and smell the roses as much as you should. This is your "smell the roses" moment, so do yourself a favor and acknowledge how much of a badass you really are. May this moment be used as gasoline for your fire. I hope the realization of how far you've come somehow propels you to strive even further.

If you aren't ready to face the challenge of your lifetime, this journey isn't for you. It's not for the weak, the entitled, or the ones filled with self-doubt. It's for the ones who believe in themselves and their God-given potential. It's for the natural-born hustlers who don't know how to unchain the ferocious tiger of entrepreneurship from their leg. I learned a long time ago that this tiger has a name too. His name is Ambo, short for Ambition, and he's not leaving me, whether I like it or not. I'm confident, so many of you can relate to this. Ambition doesn't get enough acknowledgement these days in a culture where everything is right in front of us within arm's reach. It trumps fear and uncertainty, and it's one of the greatest gifts God has ever blessed me with. It will keep you pushing forward on the narrow road no matter how many odds are stacked up against you.

I think my favorite part of the narrow road is knowing what's really on the other side of the woods. Once you make it through, you can see what's next and what lies ahead is nothing short of miraculous. Once you make it through, there's an open plain and huge mountain in sight. Below and within those mountains is the most beautiful town and community you've ever seen. There are spectacular mountains and enormous hills everywhere. Each one symbolizes a new challenge and new opportunity to climb and overcome.

But then there's that one mountain that stands taller than the rest. It gives off the energy and vibration that it's the most important mountain in the entire area. Then you can't help but look up at the peak of the mountain and fixate your gaze on the enormous structure mounted on top. There it is, in all its glory; it's the sign you've been waiting for. It's a massive bell, and it's there to change your life and business forever.

TAKE ACTION:

1. No one knows what it feels like to walk your path but you. Now's the time to take it from your mind and transfer your story onto paper. This process is healing, I promise you. Write down and describe what your narrow road looks like. Talk about how the journey started, where you are today, and what success looks like.
2. Post it on social media with the hashtags #thenarrowroad #ringthebell

CHAPTER 2:
GAZING FROM THE BOTTOM

A s you come out of the narrow road fog and can start to see things clearly again, you wipe the dust and dirt out of your eyes and realize that you have an even more amazing journey ahead.

You look around and see massive mountains everywhere. These glorious mountains overlook a beautiful, vibrant, and bustling town filled with so many people, so many businesses, and so many homes. Then you can't help but focus on the largest mountain of them all, and there's something mounted at the top of it. It appears to be the largest bell you have ever laid eyes on, and you're being drawn to it for reasons beyond your control.

That's when you realize something is burning inside of you like never before. Then it hits you. You've made it to the next level in the journey and are officially casting your vision.

My story is different from most, but if you are reading this book, then I know you have big goals and a burning desire to achieve them. You probably know what it's like to be doubted, judged, and made fun of for dreaming too big. We can't complain, though. As self-made grinders, that's what we signed up for.

Call it what it is. Being an entrepreneur can be painful, lonely, and often scary as hell. Yet somehow, we wake up day in and day out and make the conscious decision to get after our mission. I'm writing this book because I've quite literally been through hell and back, and I'm still standing here. There were 15 months of my life when I fell into complete darkness. This darkness was very real and very scary. But I made it through, thank God. Not only did I make it through, but I rose up stronger than ever in mind, body, and soul.

In my darkest moments, I became a master at self-reflection. In the moments where I felt like I was being broken down, I now realize I was actually being built up and gaining real wisdom. However, I want to keep this book less about me and more about serving you. It's intended to be a useful tool to help you level up like never before, so I'll save my detailed personal journey for another day. But I must share a little bit of a backstory so you can understand where I am coming from. After I made it through the worst moments in life, I made a promise to God that I would use the rest of my life to be a vessel to help others in every way that I could. That's why you're reading this today. I'm no guru, but I do have a certain skill set to help others become massively successful in business by leveling up their mindset and also marketing like an absolute animal.

I've always been passionate about marketing and helping other business owners succeed. When I was 19, I started a small publication with my best friend that we named Pacesetter. It goes really well with the narrative of my life. I had no money to operate, no graphic design skills, no experience in selling ad space, and no idea how to print the publication or how to logistically distribute it. Yet somehow, I begged someone at Office Depot to create the logo in return for free ad space. I begged friends, family, and any business owner I could find to let me give them ad space for whatever fee they could afford.

I called around town and found a local, family-owned printer to take a chance on us and print the publication for pennies on the dollar. Then I finally got the publications and passed them out to every shopping center, doctor's office, restaurant or business that would allow me to leave a handful at their establishment. I had no clue what I was doing, but I got it done. Pacesetter ran for a couple of years and eventually led me to my next venture.

After Pacesetter, I started a pressure washing business with my father and was back at it. He was holding down the operational side while I was doing a lot of the technician work and also holding down the business development, marketing, and sales side. So naturally, just like any hustler would do, I passed out flyers every single day. I was able to get into five neighborhoods and canvas at least one thousand flyers a day. Then I had the *brilliant* (not so brilliant) idea of supercharging my efforts with getting the word out.

That's where rollerblades came in- yes, that's right. I bought rollerblades, and instead of covering five neighborhoods, I covered ten, and instead of getting out one thousand flyers, I always got out two thousand a day or more. Oh, the joys of being young and super ambitious. In hindsight, I think about that young man and respect how badly he wanted it. I somehow gained access to gated neighborhoods with no shame and skated up and down thousands of South Florida driveways every single day without complaining. I just put my head down and executed. But I also laugh and think that was some embarrassing shit. I'm convinced I wouldn't be where I am without that piece of the puzzle in my life.

The beauty of the story is just like I had no idea how to print a local publication and be good at it, I had no idea how to advertise for a home service business. This is where the fun really started. I said to myself: "If I doubled my inbound phone calls and jobs by strapping on some rollerblades and shuffling throughout town, how can I turn up the heat and reach eight to ten thousand people a day?" That's when I bought a dirt bike and started zooming up and down every driveway I could find. I'm kidding! At this point, I heard about advertising online but had no idea what it meant or how to be successful at it.

What do you think happened next?

You know it! I went to the bookstore and bought two books, Google Ads for Dummies and SEO for Dummies. I also went back to Office Depot and bought a CD called "How To Advertise Your Business." I took the CD to the print department in the back of the store and asked the guy who made my logo if he could somehow take the CD and print out the words. I don't know what he did, but he transcribed it and told me it would cost over a hundred dollars to print it all. I should also mention that he looked at me like I was crazy and had a look on his face that screamed, who the heck prints out something like this. I had no shame, as you know. I gave him my debit card with barely any money in my account, took home those prints, and started studying day and night.

I spent the next few months with my head down in those books and also that ridiculously oversized document. I scribbled, drew circles, highlighted, and sweated on every single page during this journey of teaching myself advertising and marketing. Little did I know what was in store for me.

Side-note, if you are still in the beginning stages of your entrepreneurial journey and looking to expedite your progress, start leveraging AI aka artificial intelligence. Artificial Intelligence Apps such as ChatGPT and Bard should be used as often as possible to help you collapse time and gain as much knowledge as possible. All you do is speak or type questions or prompts into the system and you will be amazed on what comes back. It's absolutely mind-blowing and if used correctly, you will speed up your path to success.

As promised, here's a quick nugget for you. Stop thinking so small. Think really big. Andrew Carnegie once said: "You are what you think. So just think big, believe big, act big, work big, give big, forgive big, laugh big, love big, and live big." You will find out why as this chapter progresses. Don't dream big and fantasize about getting rich and flying on a plane, eating steak, and drinking champagne. Instead, envision the exact person you want to be in two years. Envision the exact type of business you want in two years. Then start operating like this person right away.

Life will eventually catch up to you. Put the throttle down hard with your personal growth, and be relentless in building an automated business as soon as possible.

♠

Campfire Chat with Expert Mountain Climber:

Tommy Mello, Owner of A1 Garage Door Service

About Tommy:

Tommy Mello is the owner and operator of A1 Garage Door Service, the host of the Home Service Expert podcast, and owner, partner, or investor in 14 other businesses ranging from home service to real estate to software. In 2007, Tommy became the sole owner and operator of a single Phoenix-based garage door service business, which came with $50,000 in debt. Today, A1Garage generates north of $120 million dollars in annual revenue, with over 500 employees in 19 states.

Tommy is a regular contributor to Inc., Entrepreneur, and other business publications on the topic of entrepreneurship and small business, as well as a sought-after podcast, radio, and television guest. When not in the office or working on the businesses, you'll find him on a plane headed to exotic destinations or chasing the little white ball around one of Arizona's many golf courses.

JM: Tommy! Good to spend time with you my brother and thanks for joining me around the campfire. The vision you have for your business is on another level. Why is casting a clear vision in business so important? How do you do it at a high level?

TM: Great to be here Jon! I'll start by saying that you must have crystal-clear vision. Even further, it must be backed by a solid plan. I hear a lot of people say: "I want to get bigger. I want to make more money, and I want to spend more time with my family." Unfortunately, that's not a good vision. You got to have the "how to" down like never before.

To simplify it, I use this golfing analogy all the time. To win, I must count the fairways, count the greens in regulation, and count my putts. An exceptional business owner must know how to win. They must know the landscape and how to dominate it from both a macro and a micro perspective. They know scalability on every level. From the labor side, they know how many technicians they need to hire. They know the KPIs they need to measure and hit. From the marketing side, they know what their conversion rates must look like and what the ROI should be dialed in at. Vision needs to be how much do I want to do this year, then what do I have to do per quarter, per month, per week for what I need to get going on today. Then think progress, progress, progress!

I truly feel like the people that don't have a clear vision will always be working harder than they need to. If they don't understand "how to" get there, they will struggle much more than they need to. The visionary needs an integrator, somebody around them that can help make it happen.

JM: I agree with your viewpoint that individuals without a clear vision will often find themselves working harder than necessary. Without a solid understanding of the "how to," they are likely to face avoidable challenges and obstacles along the way. It's also essential for visionaries to have an integrator, someone who can help bridge the gap between vision and execution, someone who can make things happen. Now, let's explore an important question: What separates good business owners from the exceptional ones?

TM: That's a great question. Exceptional business owners are always learning. They're in it to win it. They're students for life. They're identifying weaknesses. They're grabbing people that have been where they've gone. They always have somebody to lean on and ask questions. They're always reading. Leaders are readers. They're hiring consultants. They're showing up to other businesses that are bigger than them and learning how to be better.

Good business owners do good. Good business owners think they "arrived" all the time. And, you know, they're just okay. They make enough money to do okay, but they don't have that fire burning to be the biggest and the best. But exceptional business owners are relentless in being the best to have ever done it.

JM: Absolutely, I couldn't agree more with the points you've made. Exceptional business owners possess a relentless commitment to learning and self-improvement. They understand that success is not a destination, but an ongoing journey. With that in mind, I'd love to hear your insights on dominating the local market. What are the top three tips you would give to someone looking to establish their dominance in their local market?

TM: The number one tip is to get the branding perfect. I don't think enough people truly figure out their brand. Dan Antonelli is one of the best brand geniuses I've ever seen. Your truck wraps need to match your yard signs that match your mailers that match your stickers that match your website, etc. You get it! Branding is the first thing for sure.

Number two, they need to completely own Google. Google is so important. Everything from LSA to Google Business Profile to pay-per-click to the organic- the four different algorithms on Google matter.

Number three, I think the way that we recruit and train. You need all-stars to elevate your company to the next planet. You can't grow a "best in class" business with low performers. I feel like a lot of business owners recruit these guys. Then they try to train them, but the low performers don't have a want or desire to win. I was just at my cousin's shop, and he's got these guys chewing tobacco. They aren't in branded shirts. They're lazy. They only need to make $40,000 a year to survive. So when they make their $800 a week, Thursday, Friday, they're running through jobs because they have already made what they want. They don't have a real need. They don't have a burning desire that's on fire, and it shows.

So it's finding like-minded people that work hard and care about being the best. Recruit and train like-minded people consistently. If you do these three things, your dialed in pretty good. Branding, owning Google, and having an all-star team is an absolute must. Still, plenty of room to create more explosive growth, but this is a great foundation.

JM: By establishing a strong brand presence, optimizing online visibility, and recruiting like-minded individuals dedicated to excellence, businesses position themselves for sustained growth and success. However, it's important to note that while these tips create a great foundation, there is always room for continued growth and innovation. There's no doubt that building an all-star team is vital for taking a business to the next level. What are some tips to help people recruit, hire and keep talent?

TM: I recently visited an awesome restaurant. I was sitting there, and my server was such a badass. He just had a kid. He was smiling. He was funny. He was spontaneous. He was offering great service.

Let's just say that next Monday, he's doing a ride along with us. I said: "Let me tell you right now, I think you'd be perfect in my garage door company. You're a funny guy. I think you're sharp as a tack. Truthfully, I think you owe it to your wife and your newborn daughter to do a ride-along because I think you're going to make six figures."

We took a quick selfie and texted him the pic on the spot. Then I texted him and gave him a business card. Then I introduced him to my manager and got him set up on the ride-along. Let's just say my manager is in love with this guy.

He's like: "Tommy, I don't know how you did that!"

My response? "I do it all day long!" Always be recruiting. You should get your employees recruiting. Get your employees recruiting, get their wives recruiting, get their kids in their twenties recruiting. This generation will blow it up for you on social media, by the way. People always ask me how to get more jobs. I always tell them to double down on recruiting.

Don't worry so much about the jobs. You could have run half the jobs you're running with the right guys. The right guys will even make you double the money.

JM: Your ability to identify talent and seize the opportunity to recruit someone with such great qualities is amazing. I completely agree that recruiting the right individuals is crucial for business success. It's not just about filling positions; it's about finding individuals who align with your company culture, possess the right skills, and exhibit the drive to excel. Side-note, what was your reason behind the selfie?

TM: The reason I took a selfie is that I wanted him to remember who I was when he looked back into his phone and the moment we created. If I had just sent him a basic text, chances are that he would have forgotten about me. There's a high chance that when that person actually goes back to their phone, they're like, wait a minute, who is this again? So, I took a selfie, I had my company shirt, and he was smiling. It was at the restaurant. So, he recognized it. Life gets busy, and this is part of a bulletproof recruiting system, and it works.

JM: This approach definitely demonstrates a strategic and intentional approach to recruiting. It shows that you understand the importance of leaving a lasting impression and finding unique ways to stand out in a crowded marketplace. As you know, another thing businesses can do to stand out is by giving back to their communities. Why is giving back and serving so important in business?

TM: I believe that you get blessed when you bless other people, and then things come full circle. I think getting involved with the community, raising the standards of your employees, teaching them financing, helping them buy a house, and getting involved in giving back on all sorts of fronts is so important.

The fact is, from my experience, you get back ten times the return when you do stuff like this. I know your readers are wondering how this will affect their bottom line. I'll tell you that affects it really, well. If you kill a lot of birds with one stone, your people will become more charitable. You will gain more exposure which will naturally lead to more jobs. The part I really enjoy is it somehow makes you feel good about yourself and the way you conduct business. I think if everybody did a little bit more of that, we'd have a much better world to live in.

We spend two days a month, minimum, giving and serving charities with our time. We painted the YMCA, we fed kids in need, and we planted trees to help the environment. We're always intentionally serving organizations and charities. One thing I'd recommend is before you give to charity and give to the community, look in your own backyard. See if there's a person whose wife doesn't have a car. Or maybe there's a gal working for you that has bald tires and doesn't know how to get back up on her feet. Or maybe someone doesn't have a Thanksgiving dinner. I hate the companies and the owners that go to give to some random charity, like Wounded Warrior, and the gal in their company could barely feed her kids. Serving must be done from the goodness of your heart, and everything else will fall into place. Remember to always look in your own backyard first.

JM: I appreciate your perspective on the importance of giving back to the community and how it can positively impact both individuals and businesses. Your belief in the power of blessings and the concept of things coming full circle resonates strongly. It's safe to say that you're playing at an extremely high level and outpacing the competition these days. What advice would you give to your younger self to get to the promised land faster?

TM: The first thing is I would have hired consultants and asked for coaches' help way faster. Number one by far.

Number two, you know, it's the old cliche that you must work on it, not in it. I was really good at being a technician, and I probably did that way too long. Number three, I have a really big heart and probably should have had some tougher conversations and got rid of people faster. You know, hire-slow, fire-fast type of mentality.

There's a book that talks a little bit about Jack Welch and how he would top grade every year. He'd fire the bottom 10% of the majority of his company, and consistently work towards building the best team possible. I think sometimes we let good performers stay around for too long. They dictate unnecessarily, and they're prima donnas. They are the type that owns the meetings and roll their eyes too often. They are good at what they do, but they suck the life out of the company morale.

I've had to get rid of some top producers, and I wish I would have done it earlier. But in my mind, at the time when I was younger, they were paying all my bills, so I kind of had to cope with them, or I was back out in the truck. And that's just not a way to lead a company. I think the only other thing I'd say is to work on being well-funded. Try not to live paycheck to paycheck when you're starting a business because then you get captive really quickly. It's not fun when people could threaten to walk out, and you need them so badly that they can lay out all their own demands. And it's happened to me too many times. Learn from me.

JM: It's evident that you've gained a lot of wisdom along your entrepreneurial journey. Your experiences serve as valuable lessons for other business owners who can learn from your journey and make more informed decisions in their own ventures. What habits do business owners need to focus on or integrate to start absolutely crushing it?

TM: Number one is every three months go out to a successful shop, like yours. Don't be afraid to fly out of state and ask a million questions. Number two is too many people take all these notes, they go to all these seminars, and they simply don't integrate. They should put these action items on a calendar and stick to executing and implementing them like crazy. I hear too many people say that building operations manuals are so stressful. Daily meetings and performance reviews are too much work, and I don't have the time. Everybody's got a reason why they can't get started today. So, failure to implement is a big one. And then they don't know how to prioritize.

One of the best pieces of advice I could ever give is to hire an assistant. I know you have assistants, Jon, and they kill it for you. The same goes for me. Pay them well and have them do a ton of shit that you don't want to do or don't have time to do. You want someone that's detail-oriented and relationship driven. Travel often and read books and hire killer consultants. If you do those things and those things alone and you implement them- you're going to be really, really big.

JM: Such amazing advice! So one final question, Tommy before I let you go. What advice do you have for anyone who's currently climbing their own mountain?

TM: I feel like so much changed when Covid hit us. One thing I can tell you for sure is that it taught me how to reflect and grow. It taught me how to find my weaknesses and also opened my mind to more opportunities to improve. It taught me how to build an org chart and identify where I really sucked.

It really helped me figure out that my days were just flying by, and then I started looking at my calendar to see where I was spending most of my time. As you know, time is the one thing that we can't get back. So, take a notebook out and circle where you are spending most of your time. Circle things and ask yourself the hard questions. "Why were you doing that?" "How did doing this activity really help you and your business?" If you are discovering that you are doing a bunch of stuff that you shouldn't be doing, then great. Now you can figure out how to delegate those items and refocus on what matters. Things like hiring, training, orienting, etc.

Ultimately, this reflection process taught me how to build a world-class organization. You can do the same thing, but you must take the time to reflect and always be improving.

🔔

So now that I had a basic understanding of marketing and

advertising, I learned that I needed to build a website. Again, with less than a thousand dollars in my bank account, I had to do it myself as I had no money to hire anyone. Through many trials and tribulations, I learned how to design, build and host a website. I spent months working all day, pressure cleaning and pulling all-nighters learning how to optimize my basic website. After all, how well can you generate leads if you don't have a website people like? Long story short, I built every component of my first website, and it was ready to be marketed. Then the question remained: "How can I get visitors to my site with more than just flyers?" That's when I cracked open my Google Ads for Dummies book and tore through every page, trying to make something out of nothing.

I started a Google Ads account and started what would be a very long learning curve of getting things right. I wasted thousands of dollars and spent every day on the phone with GoDaddy and Google trying to get things dialed in. I treated both companies like literal business partners and most likely set the world record for calling them both more than anyone on a daily basis. Literally every day, ten times a day. Somewhere along the lines, my phone started ringing, and things were working.

During that time, I cracked open the SEO for Dummies book and applied every tip I could make sense of. Keep in mind that most of this stuff was way over my head, but I did my best. I spent more money than I had and messed up more times than I could remember in both areas, but I did it. I finally figured out how to reach eight thousand people per day. On top of my aggressive canvassing, I put my website in front of my entire county 24 hours a day, 7 days a week. That's the moment when the rocket ship took off. We went from one small pickup truck working a few days a week to seven trucks running seven days a week, day and night.

During that time, I self-taught myself more ways to turn up the heat, such as yard signs, text message marketing, relationship marketing, and more. We killed the game and sold the business years later.

That's when I started my next business adventure. I made the decision to use the trail that I blazed and turn that into a roadmap for other service companies. My thoughts were if I could just do what I did for myself and create explosive growth for other companies and unchain business owners from being a slave to the business, then I had something of value. I essentially wanted to take that thought and do the biggest thing I could mentally do at the time.

That's when I decided to start a Digital Marketing Agency that specializes in helping home service companies. You guessed it! I had absolutely no idea how to do it. I had no idea how to find clients, build and manage lots of websites, create and manage many digital marketing campaigns simultaneously or how to retain clients for years to come. Then one day, I was collecting the mail in the apartment I was living in. I noticed there was a thick envelope called ValPak in the stack, and I ripped it open. If you aren't familiar, it's the envelope that gets mailed to your house with the little advertising inserts stuffed in there. Out of the envelope fell 50 small pieces of paper, each of which was a small business advertising to the local community. A lightbulb went off, and I went back into my place to strategize. I was on to something.

The next day, I went into my office and decided to cold call every single advertiser. With no script in mind, I just called every company, mentioned that I used to own a print publication as well as a busy pressure washing company, was really strong in marketing, and to please let them give me a chance to help them market their business. Out of the 50 advertisers, 15 hung up on me, 25 didn't answer, 9 told me that they weren't the decision maker, and one actually talked to me.

The company was a grout cleaning company, and I led with authenticity and passion. In all honesty, it's the only thing I could lead with because I had no clients, no website, no logo, so business cards, and truly no idea what I was doing. That's when the kind lady said, "We've been wanting to grow our digital marketing." Then she asked when we could meet. I couldn't believe it! Someone was finally coming to meet me and talk about my services!

After what seemed to be the longest and most painfully embarrassing meeting of my life, I closed them. They offered to give me their credit card information and you guessed it, I didn't have a way to process it, so I asked if they could give me a check. They wrote me a check for $200. I shook their hands and went into my truck. I'll never forget it. I cried tears of joy, not just because of the money but because I knew God was setting me up for something big. It's been over a decade from that very moment, and since then, I've helped over a thousand businesses grow and scale their companies.

I progressively built myself into the CEO of Mr. Pipeline Internet Marketing and, along with my team, generated hundreds of millions of dollars in revenue for our clients. It's pretty special to me. What means the most is that God chose me with the responsibility to help others grow their livelihoods. Many of these clients have turned into lifelong family and friends, and it's by far one of my greatest accomplishments in life.

Why did I spend this chapter going over some of the small details of my business career? Because I want you to know why I succeeded. It all came down to one word, mindset. My mindset was growth-oriented and was operating at a strong frequency. Every expert seems to have their own interpretation of how many types of mindsets there are. To me, there are only two - fixed and growth.

People with a fixed mindset get stuck often and give up shortly thereafter. People with a growth mindset get stuck and change their approach until they get it right! Tony Robbins says it best: "Frustration is a very positive sign. It means that the solution to your problem is within range, but what you're currently doing isn't working, and you need to change your approach in order to achieve your goal."

When I started my business career, I failed plenty of times. There are three things I wish someone would have taught me sooner, which would have expedited my growth and lessened my mistakes. Those three things are a crystal clear mission statement, vision statement and core values. When these three areas are perfected, you add clarity to your purpose and help employees and customers know what your primary aim looks like.

"Frustration is a very positive sign. It means that the solution to your problem is within range, but what you're currently doing isn't working, and you need to change your approach in order to achieve your goal." Tony Robbins

A mission statement defines the company's business, its objectives and its approach to reaching those objectives. Here's an example from the beverage company Honest Tea: "To create and promote great-tasting, healthy, organic beverages." A Vision Statement describes the desired future position of the company. Here's an example from the airline company Southwest: "To be the world's most loved, most efficient, and most profitable airline."

Core Values are a set of fundamental beliefs of an organization. They are guiding principles that dictate behavior and can help people understand the difference between right and wrong. Core values also help companies to determine if they are on the right path and fulfilling their targeted goals. Your Mission Statement, Vision Statement, and Core Values can be used during interviews, performance reviews, as wall art in your office, and so much more.

If you dig this, then I have one more nugget for you. Consider adding Anti-Values to your business. For example, my company's Core Values are formed off of the acronym "FEARLESS" (Family, Excellence, Authentic, Relentless, Lion, Extraordinary Results, Service, Systems Focused). We actually have a massive mural painted on our wall that says Be Fearless. It reminds my team of what we stand for and adds some beauty to our office. Our Anti-Values are "SCARED" (Selfish, Complaining, Apathetic, Rude, Entitled, Dishonest). We don't showcase these as much as we do our Core Values, but we do use them in many ways. For example, they are showcased on our office tv slideshow and used in interviews and performance reviews all the time.

If an interviewee comes in and gives off the energy of entitlement, we dismiss the candidate immediately. If, during a performance review, one of my team members falls into the trap of complaining more often than not, we address that head-on. We'll then bring up some methods on why having a solution-based mindset over a constant complainer's mindset will do them a world of good in both life and business. Most of the time, people don't even realize they are acting a certain way, and most truly appreciate us being so *authentic* with them. See what I did there? If you haven't already, get those Core Values dialed in right away.

Back to my reason for writing this book. I want to give you a proven roadmap that will help you build and scale the business of your dreams. There are many paths that will lead you to the same destination. Just remember to leverage your mindset and work on getting mentally tough. Get excited about the process of creating thick skin and turning your adversity into your advantage. You got this. Eric Thomas tells us: "When you want to succeed as bad as you want to breathe, then you'll be successful."

Working with thousands of clients over a decade, I can tell you that I have the great privilege of having a glimpse behind the curtain.

"Get excited about the process of creating thick skin and turning your adversity into your advantage."

Jon Majak

There are a ton of things the big players in the business are doing consistently. I've analyzed their moves and integrated many of their powerhouse strategies in this book. I've helped to scale some of the best small businesses out there, in my opinion. Additionally, I've spoken with so many business owners in my life behind the scenes and come to understand why some build seven, eight and even nine-figure businesses and others crash and burn.

It all begins and ends with the *mindset*.

TAKE ACTION:

1. This chapter is all about digging deep into the treasure chest called your memory. Locate an old picture from back in the day when you were first starting your entrepreneurial journey. Whether the picture was from ten years ago or ten months ago, take notice of how far you have come from those humble beginnings. Write down and describe what that moment felt like and where you are today in your journey.
2. Post it on social media along with any relevant pictures and use the hashtags #gazingfromthebottom #ringthebell

CHAPTER 3:
WHAT DOES "RING THE BELL" MEAN?

*A**lthough the bell is far away in the distance, it captivates you more than you can ever put into words. In fact, you aren't just wondering why it's up there anymore. You made the decision to find out for yourself, so you start walking to the bottom of the mountain.*

During this moment, you start asking yourself some deep questions about the meaning of life, your purpose, how to be really successful, and how you can make a difference in this world. You start thinking about your business and how to make the very most of it. You have discovered a lot along the way and finally reached the bottom of this powerful mountain.

However, you can't help but feel as if you have more breakthroughs, you must work through. You get this overwhelming feeling that the only way you will be able to answer all of your questions is to do the impossible. It's to climb the massive mountain and ring the bell that looks like it has been silent for ages.

You start climbing the mountain that somewhat starts off like a hill. Then it progressively gets harder and steeper. You continue to ask yourself deeper and more meaningful questions. Then the self-talk starts flowing, and these questions that come rushing in all start with WHY. "Why do I feel the need to ring this bell so bad?" "Why am I doing this?"... and the ultimate question – "What's my WHY?"

🔔

I'll get right to it. When you "Ring the Bell" as loud as possible, you make more money than you ever have before, and you create an unforgettable impact in people's lives.

When you have exclusive access to some of the highest-performing home service companies in the country, you can easily see what makes them the best in their market. The obvious advantage that they have is their systemized, turn-key business. The leaders in the business have a strong mindset, clear direction, lead by example, understand the value of being "Top of Mind" and are relationship-building monsters. The administrative team is professional, courteous, empathetic, and efficient. Their sales team is second to none, and the best businesses are always employing tactics to increase their close rate. The owners and managers have a strong grip on their budget, operations, training systems, legalities, capacity, and ability to fulfill work orders at a high level.

Of course, their marketing is on fire, and the ones who shine the brightest have a social impact component embedded into their organization. Essentially, the strongest businesses don't just focus on money; they focus on making an impact internally within their culture and also externally within their community. As Henry Ford once said: "A business that makes nothing but money is a poor business."

I have come to understand that a local market leader's strength lies not only in what they do for their customers but also in their ability to create impact in and out of the organization. I like to call this: Mission Driven Leadership. It's extremely important that you understand this book is not designed to be some "fufu granola give away everything to everybody" BS. It's about getting the bag and being a money magnet. It's about generating so many work orders and invoices that you need a team to keep track of it all. It's about getting paid. Because if you get paid at a high level, your resources will overflow, and if you channel them right, you can do a world of good in life.

Let's get visual for a moment. If you can hold onto this vision every day you operate, your life will never be the same. Envision yourself owning a business in this town and living in a mountainside community or village where there are a ton of houses, buildings, and people everywhere. Now, glance into the distance and notice the tallest mountain top in that village. On top of that mountain is a huge 80-foot bell mounted where everyone can see it. Have you ever seen pictures of the enormous Christ the Redeemer statue mounted in Rio de Janeiro, Brazil? Now take a second and picture something enormous and ancient but, more than anything, powerful and prominent. Anyone who is lucky enough to catch a glimpse of this bell understands there must be quite the story behind it.

"A business that makes nothing but money is a poor business."

Henry Ford

As you know, the beginning of each chapter touches on segments of the climb to the top. Here is the full story; I know you can't close your eyes right now, but that doesn't mean you can't dial into your imagination. Here we go. Can you see this vision of staring at the bell from the bottom as clear as day? It might take you a minute. Then it will hit you. When the time is right, you now need to picture yourself taking a deep breath and charging up this mountain over, past, under, and around every obstacle that stands in the way on the journey to the top.

It's a long trek up, and you only stop when you absolutely need a moment to recalibrate and refocus. Perhaps you even pump the brakes to recharge and gain strength and wisdom near a campfire. Then you get back to it. Up, over, and around more obstacles. Then the climb stops and you hit a wall, literally. That's right, you look up and see at least another thousand feet of the scariest vertical climb ahead of you. You feel like it's over. You start to get delirious and your will to fight lessons immediately. You feel like it's impossible.

Then you remember the famous quote from Nelson Mandela, who

spent 27 years in prison fighting for what he believed in: "It always seems impossible until it's done." That's when you understand there are levels to real success.

This is the point where the uphill trek is done and the straight rock wall climb ascension begins. Another deep breath and you push, despite your painful self-talk. One breath and one long arm extension at a time, you climb. Finally, you're there. You've pushed harder than you ever have before, and you've reached the very top of the mountain. You're winded and every ounce of strength seems to have left your body. Your tank's literally just about empty and your body is tired from fighting the good fight. Somehow the only item left in your tank is gratitude. You are full of pure thankfulness that you still have breath in your lungs, and you somehow persevered your way to the top. You look over in complete and utter amazement. You then make your way over to the greatest sight you've ever seen. The Bell. It's bigger than you would have ever imagined from the bottom of the mountain. It's old, very worn down, and screams that it's full of heart, yet, it also looks like it hasn't made a sound in ages. Hanging from the bell is a huge woven rope with a massive steel object in the middle.

That's when you collect your thoughts and realize why you were so compelled to get to the top. You realized that if you rang it like crazy, everyone would have no choice but to look up and notice you. For better or for worse, people were going to have no choice but to know you exist. That's when you decide it's time. It's time to make the most noise you've ever made in your entire life. You then dig your heels into the ground to set a steady foundation and brace yourself for the unknown. You take both hands, grip the bottom of the old rope, and you ring the bell as hard as you possibly can. In your mind, you sound the alarms, smashing the gong and literally crushing the bell with every ounce of your being.

Ring! Ring! Ring! Ring! Ring!

You do this for quite some time until your hands are bleeding, and every single person in the town is looking up at you in complete awe.

That's the moment you let go and fall to the floor in complete exhaustion. That's the moment you stake your claim. That's the moment when everyone in town knows you exist.

You're completely exhausted, and when you get up, you take a moment to breathe and reflect. You take a moment to be intentional and celebrate a new and major success that you fought hard for. Then you start trekking back down into town and notice your shirt is ripped into shreds by the jagged mountainside and thorn-filled bushes. It must have torn on the way to the top. That's when you rip a straggled piece off and dig your bloody fingers into the dry dirt. You sketch an outline of your brand onto it and decide you're going to climb to the top of the bell.

After all, you made it this far. Why not tie it to the top of the bell in complete and utter glory?

You did what most considered impossible. You then gather your thoughts and look down from the top. People are still staring and continue to look up in complete awe. Everyone now knows you exist and realizes that you will do whatever it takes to be seen and heard. It's nothing short of miraculous.

"Ring the bell means that you will do whatever it takes to make noise so that you can make as much money as possible while leaving a lasting impact."

When the bell rings, it symbolizes forcing a sound on people's ears that they have no choice but to listen to you. If they hear you, they will be forced to know you exist. If they know you exist, you can get in front of them. If you get in front of them, you can help them solve their needs through the service you offer in exchange for money. The other component of ringing the bell is all about leaving a lasting impression and a memorable impact on people's lives. If you ring the bell as loud and as crazy as possible, you will force an unforgettable moment into people's minds. They will always remember that madman or mad woman who was brave enough to stand out and be heard in order to leave a lasting impression. If you do it right, they will remember you for the rest of their lives.

When you ring the bell for money, it's self-explanatory as you offer a service with the end result being more revenue added to your top line. When you ring the bell to make an impact on people's lives, there's more intention that needs to be integrated. You must be super intentional in terms of showing up to those who need it most. Sometimes it will be your employees; other times, it will be a local charity. Sometimes it will be vendors, and other times it will be your industry friend or a competitor that just needed a break or a helping hand. Essentially, one part is ringing for revenue, and the other is ringing to serve and care for the ones who need it most.

Here's a pro tip for you that I want you to take from me. Before you start smashing the bell, get yourself an extra pair of hands to help you. Perhaps it could be someone on your current team who has the ability to take on more work, or other options include a new hire such as an Executive Assistant, Personal Assistant, Virtual Assistant, or Marketing Specialist. Trusting the right mind to be by your side to help you through the struggles and help you advance your mission with velocity is priceless. I promise you that this extra "expense" will pay for itself immediately.

Anyone can start a business and earn a few dollars to put in their pocket. Not everyone can use their status and position of power to help others; that's the difference. When your life is over, do you want to be known as the entrepreneur who made it to the top and just looked out for yourself? Or do you want to be the person who made it to the top, made a ton of money, helped as many people as possible, and made a lasting difference in the world? I'll be completely transparent with you. It's not the easier option, but it's the one that will fill you with so much gratitude and fuel your purpose beyond belief.

Pausing to reflect and look inside my backpack: A quick look into my story and the importance of having a WHY.

Everyone has a different story or baggage they carry in their backpack of life. One of the most important mindset lessons I can teach you is to open the bag and look right into it. Don't run from your past adversities, but rather be as bold as a lion and face them head-on. Then once you face them, you are one step closer to defeating them. How do you obliterate the weight you've been carrying on your shoulders for so long? You must start by defining your "why" and then fuel it by relentlessly charging forward and never looking back.

Here's what I mean; For me, I ring the bell because I want to create the life of my dreams for my family and also because I want to make an impact before my time is done on this beautiful spinning rock called Earth. To take it further, my why is defined as: "To show up for God, myself and the ones I love most." It's really important to lean into this question of "why" you ring the bell for a moment. The reason being is that business gets really hard, really fast. Anyone who tells you differently is pulling the wool over your eyes and bullshitting you.

Whether I've learned this through my own self-discovery or through coaching some of the most incredible people in the home service business, I've come to see one thing really clearly. The difference between those who kill it and grow like crazy and someone who fizzles away comes down to a really strong "why" and re-shifting focus to it when life crushes them. Trust me; it's not if life crushes you; it's when. It's in those moments of uncertainty that you must envision your reason for driving so hard and figure out how to play through the pain. I'll get deep with you for a moment.

For example, my wife got injured after she received her first dose of the Covid vaccine in January of 2021. I mean, really sick. She got her vaccine when they first rolled out and started feeling unwell right away. The sick feeling never left and then hit a peak a month or so later. Things progressed, and she ended up losing the use of her legs and had to get taken away in an ambulance in the middle of the night.

Unfortunately, as I'm writing this book, she is still suffering, and it's been a few years since she got her shot. She has had bouts of vertigo, extreme fatigue and found herself bedridden more often than not. In the past, I had to often take on the role of mom, dad, caretaker, and more without hesitation. Slow improvement is happening but we aren't out of the woods quite yet. All in Gods timing. I tell you all this because I want to drive home the importance of knowing your "why."

I have every reason in the world to be depressed and down, but I choose not to be that way. The reason is that every time my brain starts to feel the pain of my reality, I envision a picture of my wife, son, and myself hugging each other tightly. Remember how I told you the importance of holding onto small visions? This is one of the reasons. My family is my primary "why" – they are my reason. A "why" written on paper is completely worthless; however, when you put it into action, the power unfolds right in front of you. That's why I play through the pain and relentlessly strive to be a force for good for my wife, my son, and the ones I love most.

In addition, here's a further glimpse into why I'm so motivated personally. For some reason, there is this burning desire within me to try my best when I go in on something. These days, the reason I ring the bell louder than ever is that I want to create a life for my family that I never had. I grew up without much money, primarily raised by a single mom. Born in Baltimore, Maryland, she took me to Florida when I was 3 to live a better life away from the adversity I was born into. We lived with my grandparents in an elderly person's neighborhood in Delray Beach, FL, before she eventually saved up enough money to move us into an apartment complex. I lived there for years. Some would call it the struggle. I guess I would too.

Years passed by, and I remember my mom and I moving in with

some guy who eventually abused her right in front of me. For one quick second, imagine being an innocent, protective little child watching his mom get smacked around by some alcohol-infused degenerate. It changes the way you see the world, that's for sure. I'm not really certain how long this went on, to be honest. My therapist said my brain blocked out those memories as some sort of coping mechanism. Somehow we made it out of that disaster alive and into an apartment and eventually a townhouse.

My mom was a secretary and worked all the time to try to create a better life for us. We never had much, but we had a roof over our head, clean clothes, and each other. When Christmas or birthdays came around, she got me a small gift or two, but it always ended with her saying: "I'm sorry, I know you wanted more, but I don't have anything left in my checking account." During those times, I smiled and said: "It's ok, ma, I understand." But underneath my halfhearted smile, I was hurting.

Truthfully, my childhood was filled with moments just like this. I could go on for a bit, but I only really want to get into another cornerstone moment in my life so we can get back to business. I know I must mention the next part because it's important you know who I am through and through. Hopefully, showing you my cards will inspire you to use your struggle as a roadmap to help others.

So it's hard to write this down, but I wouldn't be serving you at the highest level if I didn't keep it real with you as I promised at the opening of this book. So I'll stick to my word and be an open book to you. I have also made it through hell on earth and survived complete darkness. I am a suicide survivor. Yes, that's right, I made it through literal hell, and somehow I'm living to tell you about it. In fact, I lived in what they call a suicidal trance for just about over a year. I tried to end my life a handful of times but God had bigger plans. I want to take this moment to speak for all of my fallen brothers and sisters who didn't make it through and tell you that they most likely never wanted to die. They just didn't want to suffer anymore. I never wanted to die. In fact, I tried really, really hard to stay alive. I just couldn't take it anymore.

Leading up to the first time I attempted it, ending my life was never a thought. In hindsight, I know exactly what happened to me to create this moment. My wife had a traumatic birth experience when delivering our son and almost passed away after he was born. Two days after we got home from the hospital, she was shaking uncontrollably. On the second night, she looked at me and said: "Jon, I feel like I'm dying." I couldn't process those words and went numb. Then once I was able to absorb it, I told her to call the doctor right away. Well, this was in the middle of the night, and the doctor told her to take her vitals.

Through speaker phone, I heard the doctor tell my wife: "Lauren, your shaking isn't normal. You might be having a stroke, and if you don't get to the hospital within minutes, you might not make it." Then I grabbed my sleeping few-day-old son from his crib and put both of them in the car. I ran every light and what should have been a 40 minute drive took us about 15 minutes. When we arrived, I dropped her off at the front, where nurses were waiting for her. I then parked and looked in the backseat to see my precious boy. He was wearing a onesie, and it was freezing out. That's when I looked at him and prayed to God. Then I looked at my son and said: "We got this, Cam, we came here as a unit of 3, and we will leave as a unit of 3."

Because we had rushed, we didn't have the right clothes on, and it was really cold out. So I took my shirt off and wrapped him up, and we courageously walked into the hospital. When we got to the room, there had to be eight people screaming to keep Lauren alive. The pads were out, and they were trying all sorts of medicines and methods to keep her alive. That's when they told me to sit. That's when one of the doctors looked at me and said, "We are so glad you're here. We are going to give it everything we have to keep your wife alive."

That was a moment I'll never forget. That was the moment that officially pushed me over the edge. Because of that simple statement, my head fell down into my lap, and I started seeing stars. My vision literally turned black then I saw swirling stars fading away into the distance. You have all heard about a heartbreak. Well, this is what was happening to me, but it wasn't my heart - it was my mind. My mind broke at that exact moment.

It was like the perfect storm hit me because during this stage of my life, I was also seeking professional help to attempt to heal from my childhood trauma. I wanted to be the best man possible when my newborn son arrived. Little did I know, I was just ripping open repressed wounds further, vulnerably inviting in more pain.

I guess 30-something years of massive toxic stress combined with watching my wife almost die in front of me is what it took for the bend to finally turn into a break.

By the grace of God, these incredible medical professionals saved my wife's life. A week or so later, we walked out of there as a unit of 3 and tried to get back to life the best we could. It was a tough recovery journey for her. It was a tough recovery journey for me. Behind the scenes, I was broken. So broken that I downward spiraled, and there was no saving me. I became disengaged from all of the beauty this amazing world had to offer.

Then for the next year or so, I spent most of my time trying to come up for air. Each time the final moment came closer and closer. The last time was something out of a movie scene. I wrote my goodbye letter, left it in my closet, and walked into my driveway. It was raining, thundering, and lightning harder than I could put into words. I sat in my truck and cried. Then I prayed. I took one final deep breath before making my final move, and then something miraculous happened at the last second. The torrential rain turned off like a light switch was controlling it. I knew at that moment that I was saved, and my life was spared. God spoke to me that night and demanded I keep a promise to him.

In so many words, I was told that I hadn't understood the meaning or purpose of my life. Up to that point, I simply worked hard and had the motivation to do my best. He said where I must live and breathe in absolute dedication. Dedication to him and the ones that I love most. It clicked for me, and I then made the biggest commitment of my life. I promised and cried out that I would spend the rest of my life telling people that He's right there with us in every moment, whether our human minds realize it or not. I also made a promise that I would be forever *dedicated* to being a force for good in life.

That's why you're reading this book right now. My mission has nothing to do with book sales. Believe it or not, I could actually care less about how much revenue comes in. The metric I care about is how many people did I inspire to build the business of their dreams and live a life of purpose and dedication.

🔔

Here's a quick look at why I'm so motivated professionally. I feel like being a small business owner is a true privilege that shouldn't be taken for granted. People often say: "Support Small Business" or "Shop Small Business," which is amazing - but in all fairness, I like to look at the other side of the coin as well. Why should we expect educated consumers to spend their hard-earned money with us when they have so many choices in life? The answer is simple, in my opinion. Give them a reason to support you other than just fulfilling your service. If small businesses are just generating a pure profit and pocketing it, then why should we expect people to only shop small? However, if these businesses are giving back to their community and serving others locally in a selfless way, then it's a completely different story.

My humble opinion is that we, as entrepreneurs, should be using our power and influence for good and for change. The Bible says it best in Matthew 5:14, "Be the Light." Something special happens when your business embeds some sort of social impact component. You get the opportunity to help the ones you care for most and also those in need. For example, there are local organizations in need, such as homeless shelters, animal shelters, foster care organizations, and more.

The world needs more leaders and people who do more good, especially in today's crazy day and age. I believe private giving should be kept private. For example, if you tithe consistently at church or selflessly give food away to a homeless person in need, that moment should most certainly be between you, God, and the recipient. Public giving is different and should be public for many reasons, which we will unpack further as our journey together continues. Let's just say that public giving is a blessing in more ways than I can truly put into words, but here's a little glimpse.

When your customers find out you donate a portion of your profit, they treat you differently. When your employees understand that you lead with integrity and genuinely care about helping others, the energy massively changes for the better in your company. This is what I like to call the ripple effect of ringing the bell. Some would say it's the best part of making so much noise. "People respond to energy much more than they do to words. They respond to what they feel. Energy, spirit, transfer of energy is what people respond to." Ed Mylett.

We currently do a lot of great things within Mr. Pipeline, but one of my favorites is knowing we support local organizations that are doing so much good in this world. To get your wheels turning, I'll go over a few different ways we strive to make a difference. For example, many military service members leaving the service have a hard time transitioning into civilian life. Not only are they faced with the challenges of their visible and unseen injuries, but they are also overwhelmed with trying to navigate their way into the civilian workforce and can experience financial difficulties when trying to provide for themselves and their families. We support an organization called Wounded Veterans Relief Fund, which solely exists to provide emergency financial support to disabled veterans. Saving lives and keeping families together is their mission, and it's our privilege to support them. Learn more about how you can contribute at www.wvrf.org.

The second organization we support is called Place of Hope. Place of Hope is a faith-based children's organization providing family-style foster care (emergency and long-term); family outreach and intervention; maternity care; safety for victims of domestic minor sex trafficking; transitional housing and support services for youth aging out of foster care; housing and support services for homeless families; foster care recruitment and support; hope and healing opportunities for children and families who have been traumatized by abuse and neglect. Partnering with this incredible organization means a lot to our company. We take a vested interest in creating gifts for the children around the holidays, and our team has a lot of fun with it. Learn more about how you can contribute at www.placeofhope.com.

Last but certainly not least, the third organization we support is called The Miracle League. The Miracle League removes the barriers that keep children with mental and physical disabilities off the baseball field and lets them experience the joy of America's favorite pastime. The Miracle League is about making new friends, building self-esteem, and being treated just like other athletes. The bonds that are formed can't fully be described. The Miracle League serves children and adults who suffer from any physical or mental disabilities, which causes them to be excluded, whether intentionally or not, from conventional Baseball leagues. This is one special cause; once again, it's our privilege to help them in any way we can. Learn more about how you can contribute at www.miracleleague.com.

"People respond to energy much more than they do to words. They respond to what they feel, not what they hear and see. Hearing and seeing are real low-level influences. Energy, spirit, transfer of energy is what people respond to."

Ed Mylett

The truth of the matter is that we are all in business to make money. We must make money and create a healthy profit to scale and serve. Otherwise, we would be out of business, and there wouldn't be a bell to ring. Some of us want to be filthy rich, some of us just want nice toys, some of us want to be financially free, and some of us just want to be comfortable and save for retirement. I have zero judgment toward whichever road you choose. To each their own. Whatever you choose, you must understand the work that goes into creating the lifestyle you desire.

For me, I love knowing our company makes exceptional money and also gets to be a light in others' lives. When one of my team members tells me they are moving into a new home, buying a new car, traveling somewhere new, etc., I light up. To me, I get the most satisfaction knowing I'm making a difference during my short stay on this beautiful planet. If you want to build a business full of substance and a non-stop engine for real change, you must do more than just earn money. You must contribute and make a real difference in this world.

Tony Robbins says that "the greatest key to a happy life is to contribute." He has dedicated his life to giving to others. From initiating programs in over 1,500 schools and providing fresh water to 100,000 people a day in India to ensuring nuns in San Francisco have a place to operate their soup kitchens, Tony's actions demonstrate his belief that when we give more, we become more. You can do this in the form of volunteering, donating, serving, or in many other ways.

To keep driving the value, here are a few more reasons why it's so important to embed a giving aspect into your business. The first reason is that when you give without expectations, amazing energy is put into the world. It always comes back to you tenfold. The second reason is when you give to a local food bank, donate toys to children in need, and such, you are doing God's work.

You are loving and serving, and it feels good. The third reason is that when you embed a social impact into your business, your customers notice. In a world full of small businesses that blend in, be a business that shines bright and stands out like no other. How do you do that? You create a page on your website called: Giving Back. On that page, you list the cause(s) you support and why. Then you list how people can support you. Then you share it on social media and continue to build off your mission year after year. According to Forbes, their Global Study reveals consumers are four to six times more likely to purchase, protect and champion purpose-driven companies.

The fourth reason is that at the heart of every great company is a culture that's on fire. I've seen it firsthand when I say something exceptional happens internally within your company when you give back. Your team is always looking and sees that you are not about pocketing every dollar of profit. They see a giver, a provider, a servant leader, and a caring and loving human being. They see someone that isn't a boss but a real leader they can look up to. That's what it's all about. It's all about building a strong business that makes money and makes people feel good as often as possible. If you've done that, you've clearly hit the objective. You understood the mission and privilege of being a business owner.

TAKE ACTION:

As you can probably tell by now, I don't like formalities. I like to play by my own rules, and that's why I'm going to task you with two action items for this chapter.

Action Item #1

1. What's your reason for pushing so hard? Take a moment and define your "Why"
2. When you are done, post your why along with a coinciding picture on social media with the hashtags #mywhy #ringthebell

Action Item #2

1. Add a page to your website and label it "Giving Back." List 1-3 organizations that mean something to you. Don't rush this process. Take your time and do what's necessary to unlock what matters most to you. Place a few sentences about why this organization matters so much to your business and publish the page. (Make sure to get consent from the organization as well.)
2. When you're done, post the page on social media and explain who you are taking a stand for and why. Don't forget to include the hashtags #givingback #ringthebell

If you are finding value so far in this book, please take 60 seconds to write a quick review on Amazon.

As you know by now, this book is completely dedicated to helping you grow both personally and professionally.

The greatest thing I can ask for in exchange for the value of the book is a review. Gaining great reviews helps the algorithms showcase Ring the Bell over others. The more this book gets seen, the more impact it will deliver.

Thank you.

CHAPTER 4:

WHO YOU RING IT TO

Y our climb continues, and the longer you ascend, the harder it becomes, both mentally and physically. Your mental toughness is reaching new heights, and it seems like your ego fades away into the abyss.

You are not only thinking about yourself anymore but reflecting on reasons much deeper. Who am I even ringing this bell to? What am I trying to tell them? Your mind is tired, but the fire inside of you is relentless, and you charge on. You sit down to rest and catch your breath; your body is trying to quit on you.

That's when you notice that the steep hill just stops suddenly. The deep incline immediately turns into a straight vertical climb of pure rock. The best part is you've never rock-climbed in your life, but that doesn't stop you. You start to feel truly alive as you grip fearlessly onto the rigid rock. Your head turns up; you take a deep breath and begin to climb like you've never climbed before.

🔔

Customers are the lifeblood of any small business. Without them, nothing else is even possible. Just be mindful of this statement forever-everyone is not your perfect customer.

It took me a long time to understand this because I wanted to drastically grow my revenue year over year. I found out the hard way that they're just some people that you weren't meant to do business with. You have to find the humor in that statement! We all know that one customer that you wish you had never serviced. Their attitude, the way they treated you, the amount they paid, the expectations they had, it's borderline unforgettable! But they exist for a reason, and that reason is to tell you who your ideal customer is and isn't. I believe you also go through this experience so you can know the customer you never want to be when people serve you in your personal life.

As you brainstorm this moment, understand that there are some other things to consider during this phase. This is also the time to start sharpening your blade on your competitive advantage. Are you a veteran? Then make a mental note of it because soon it will be time to really drive this home on your branding and into your culture. Are you a woman or minority-owned business? Then now is your time to embed that important piece into your avatar. Why? Because people buy from people they relate to and that they like. Plus, it gives you an extra bullet in your chamber to beat out a competitor, which I love!

The million (or multi-million) dollar question is: Who do I ring the bell to make the most money possible?

The million (or multi-million) answer is: Your perfect customer avatar.

How to define your perfect customer avatar:

It's easy to sit back and think about who your ideal customer is. It's hard to intentionally carve out time to know who your customer is at the deepest level. Like my friend Josh Latimer always says: "Do Hard Things."

Take your time with this process because once it's done, it's time to get in front of them like never before. It's time to get to work. Before we map out your perfect customer or customer avatar, I advise doing some due diligence on your local market. Understanding the local population's key data points really matters. This short discovery process will help you understand how large or small your market is as well as how many of your perfect customers exist and what zip codes they reside and/or work in. You can find this out from a quick Google search and by looking up local Census information in and around your headquarters. Next, let's start by envisioning what your perfect customer looks like and giving them a name. In this example, I will say that my perfect customer is a middle-aged male named Joe.

"Everyone is not your perfect customer."

Jon Majak

Next, let's peel back a layer and define their education level, location, relationship status and household income. In this example, I will say Joe is college educated and lives in Palm Beach County, FL. He is also married and has a combined household income of $175k or more.

Next, let's peel back a few more layers on who your perfect customer is at their core. That's where we need to define his personality type, values, online and offline hangouts and needs/desires. In this example, I will say that Joe is an easygoing man who values honesty, kindness and a job well done. He spends time online on Facebook, searching on Google, browsing Reddit and enjoys the neighborhood apps. He spends his time offline at outdoor events, the church and also at the gym. He needs the basics, such as water, food, and shelter. He desires to inspire others and to always be a good neighbor, friend and family member.

Next, where does your perfect customer historically search for their home service needs? In this example, Joe searches on Google, Facebook and local print publications.

Now make sure you work through this exercise yourself and document your answer. Label it your "Customer Avatar" or your "Perfect Customer."

Campfire Chat with Expert Mountain Climber:

Dave Carroll, CEO of DOPE Marketing

About Dave:

Dave Carroll is the founder and CEO of DOPE Marketing. DOPE Marketing helps businesses automate laser-focused direct mail to the neighbors of their jobs. DOPE Marketing's bolt on direct mail service makes life simple by sending automated direct mail with their open API, Zapier integration and direct connection with CRMs like Housecall Pro, Customer Factor and Jobber.

DOPE Marketing has a tool called Neighborhood Blitz, where you can draw a shape on a map and send laser-focused postcards with no minimum order to any neighborhood in the United States. This service is great for home service, agencies, e-commerce and local businesses.

DOPE's software allows you to send direct mail within seconds that will deliver anywhere in the country within 3 to 5 days. You can also order any print or marketing items that your business requires with short turnover and low minimums. Dave and his team are leading the industry in direct mail and print automation. They are very focused on changing the way that agencies and businesses look at direct mail. No longer are the old days of "spraying and praying" with direct mail. Laser-focused, trigger-based direct mail is the way of the future!

JM: What's up Dave! Thank you for joining me around the campfire, it's always a pleasure. I admire everything you and your business stand for. The way your company helps to zero in on the perfect customer avatar is incredible. Where should Home Service Pros start when figuring out who to laser-target?

DC: The best guide of who to laser target is finding the D.O.P.E in your business; the Data On Previous Engagement. Thankfully, there's an easier way to do this.

Go to your CRM and download your customer list from last year. Take that list into an excel spreadsheet and highlight the entire list. Sort the list by the ZIP Code column. You should now have the list of jobs you did last year in order by ZIP Code. Make a list of the top three ZIP Codes where you did work last year. This is the exact area where you should be focused on!

Think about why you have more jobs in the ZIP Codes. Maybe that's one of the ZIP Codes where your house is. Maybe that's the neighborhood you grew up in. Maybe you have a customer in that area that gives you a lot of referrals. No matter what the reason is, let your data show you where you should be spending your time and your marketing dollars.

Data will always tell a story; you just need to know where to look. Your customers will guide you in the right direction.

JM: Data is a powerful tool that can reveal patterns and trends, providing a clear story about your customers and their preferences. Why should business owners leverage data rather than just winging it or going off their gut when targeting people?

DC: The beautiful thing about Data is that numbers don't lie. Success leaves clues, and the data in your business can show you how to make decisions that are not based on emotions, but based on facts.

The thing about homeowners is that they cluster. People like to live in the same neighborhood as other people that they have things in common with. Do you think that someone making $40,000 a year who can't afford your services is going to live in a neighborhood next to another family living in a $500,000-plus house that needs the work your company specializes in? Probably not…

As business owners, we are emotional creatures. We are put in a position to make a lot of different decisions, we need to trust our gut, and we need to make sure that we are focused on the right things during the day. Focusing on data allows you to make fact-based decisions as opposed to emotional decisions or conclusions that are based off of "well it just seems like that would make sense."

The exercise we discussed previously about taking your current customer list and using that list to make educated decisions on marketing dollars is one of the best examples of how ANY business owner can use data in their business.

JM: You've highlighted a crucial aspect of business decision-making—relying on data rather than solely on emotions. How should Home Service Companies be leveraging direct mail like an absolute monster?

DC: The best way to leverage direct mail is to make sure that the neighbors of current jobs are getting reminded about what's happening in their neighborhood. The old method of "spray and pray" just doesn't work anymore. In the past, companies would send huge Postcard Mailings and spend thousands or even tens of thousands of dollars spraying postcards all over town and then praying that they would get enough of a result to cover the enormous cost of the mailing. Thankfully, there's a better way. Harvard Business School did a study that said it takes 7 to 11 touches for a consumer to remember a brand. Thankfully direct mail is one of the highest-value touches in any marketing campaign because you're literally putting a message in someone's hand. Ideally, the postcards are designed to look the exact same as your website, your truck wrap, your Facebook Ads, and every other "touch" that a homeowner might see from your company. Think about the workflow in your business. You get a lead; you give an estimate, the estimate is approved, the work is scheduled, the work is completed, and the work is paid for. The idea is that the neighbors of that job should be educated along this entire workflow.

"Your neighbor is about to get their siding cleaned."

"Be on the lookout; we're going to be in the neighborhood."

"Pardon the dust, pardon the noise, we are working in the area."

"Check out the job we just finished in your neighborhood."

Create designs that match your brand guideline and educate the neighbors about jobs and tell them about the amazing work you're doing in their neighborhood.

Direct mail is intimate and memorable, especially when it follows the look and feel of your other marketing campaigns.

JM: You've raised an important point about leveraging direct mail effectively by targeting the neighbors of current jobs and providing consistent messaging throughout the customer journey. Building upon this idea, another powerful marketing tool to consider for local businesses is yard signs. These signs have the potential to create a strong visual presence and attract attention within the community. What are the best ways to kill it with Yard Signs?

DC: When you're putting out yard signs, there's a couple of different strategies that I've learned over the years. Everyone knows that you should put a sign in front of the house where you just did a job. That's a no-brainer.

Know if you really want to get aggressive and be a ninja, I've got some pretty DOPE strategies for you.

My favorite place to put yard signs is coming out of busy gas stations. Find a gas station in a busy area where there is a stop sign coming out of the parking lot and then another stop sign on the street. People are "mentally checked out" when they enter the gas station, but after they gas up, they are ready to get back to life. Remind them that they have been meaning to use a service like yours so when they pull out of the gas station and hit that stop sign, the first thing they see is a yard sign with your company, your phone number and maybe even a QR code for them to scan.

Another strategy I really like is targeting the off-ramps of busy freeway exits. Think of the exits or people getting off to go to the "nice or affluent" areas in town. Maybe it's an exit that can sometimes take two lights to get through. Put 1-yard sign right up by the stoplight and another yard sign maybe 10 or 15 car lengths back. This allows you to get two touches from each potential customer and, depending on the exit, hundreds, thousands or maybe even tens of thousands of views per day. Other places that I love to place yard signs are coming out of Home Depot, high-end grocery stores, places like Target or HomeGoods, or other places where homeowners shop. The great part about this strategy is that the employees of these businesses don't care that your yard signs are in the parking lot, making them stay up a bit longer and get you some more jobs. One thing to remember is the harder it is to place a sign, the harder it is to remove that sign.

My cleaning company goes pretty hard with Signs. I try to get out at least 50 to 100 per week during the slow season and upwards of 200 per week during the busy season. It's one of the main ways we grew our business when we first started.

Depending on how aggressive you want to get, strategically placing yard signs can be a great form of lead generation.

JM: You've shared some effective strategies for maximizing the impact of yard signs as a form of lead generation. Placing signs in front of houses where you've completed jobs is a common practice, but you've taken it a step further with some DOPE strategies. I love your line: "Come at them from every angle!" What tips do you have to help Home Service Pros absolutely dominate their local market?

DC: The biggest thing you need to remember is that people buy from companies that they trust. Think about what you can do to get a potential customer or homeowner to trust your company.

One thing I live by is that "good marketing breeds trust."

If you look like 1 million bucks, smell like 1 million bucks, talk like 1 million bucks, what's the difference between you and a company that's been open for 30 years? The answer is nothing. If you simply provide a quote, show up, do what you're saying you're going to do, and don't collect the check until your job is done, you're exactly the same as a business in your area that's been around forever. Perception outweighs reality, but a first impression lasts forever. Make sure that instead of running some crazy shotgun marketing campaigns all over town that instead, you are focused on specific areas or neighborhoods. Go back to the Harvard Business School study of the 7 to 11 touches; instead of touching a bunch of different customers two or three times, be intentional and focus on specific neighborhoods where you can grow your brand and educate the RIGHT customers for your business.

JM: You've highlighted the crucial role that trust plays in attracting customers to your business. Building trust is definitely essential, and as you mentioned, solid marketing can foster that trust. I'm curious to learn more about your company's involvement in giving back and supporting other organizations. Does your company give to or help other organizations?

DC: One thing is very important to me because my background is focusing on helping to lower the recidivism rate for people coming out of prison, halfway houses or treatment centers.

In our print shop, we focus on hiring people coming out of adverse situations to give them an opportunity for employment so they can get back on their feet. If you know anyone coming out of a hard time, please don't hesitate to connect them with our team so we can help point them in the right direction for some assistance.

JM: That's super inspiring my man. You are making a difference, that's for sure. One last question for you Dave, before we put out the campfire. What advice do you have for anyone who is currently climbing their own mountain?

DC: I remember over the first couple of years of starting my cleaning company, I would be so tired at the end of the day. My back was screaming from throwing around ladders all day. My hands would smell like a window cleaning bucket. I wasn't making very much money. I remember thinking, "this isn't what I signed up for…"

One of the best pieces of advice I ever got was when I was talking to a mentor of mine, and he said to me, "Dave, what will get you through the hard days is remembering your why."

You need to think about why you started your business. Why you are doing what you're doing. Why you wake up with excitement about being able to provide opportunities to your employees, improve the value of your clients' homes with your services, and do something that you love to do during the day.

Knowing your why and understanding that no matter how hard today is, how a job goes or how stressful things get, you started this business because you are now in control of your own destiny, and that's a powerful thing.

You made the decision to go get a Tax ID and open your company and that is a big responsibility. If running a business was easy, everyone would be doing it. But only you know why you made that decision. Every time things get hard, focus on that "why" and remind yourself that you're doing an amazing fucking job.

🔔

Now that you nailed down a clear picture of your perfect customer to ring the bell to for money, we need to define who we ring the bell to in order to maximize your impact in life.

The next major question is: Who do I ring the bell to for maximum impact?

The answer is: Your perfect team and your perfect organizations. So now we need to spend a moment defining what that looks like.

Dialing in on these answers really adds a lot of clarity to your mission in life and business. I've found that once you do the hard work of discovering exactly what this looks like, something huge happens.

Your purpose becomes crystal clear. Somehow your purpose starts to walk on two legs as well because you're nurturing and feeding it. It takes on a life of its own, and it's almost impossible to pump the brakes on it once it's moving. The best way to start this process is to write things down. I always say, on paper on purpose. Open up the notepad on your phone or take out a piece of paper and start brainstorming about the people and organizations that matter the most to you in life.

First, I must start by saying that I've worked with thousands of business owners in my career. I have zero judgment but I find it mind-blowing that most of them don't make any real time for themselves. The reason being is that I was one of those owners for over 20 years. I literally never thought of myself or the importance of taking care of my mind, body and soul. It wasn't until I almost lost my life that I got the picture. Between that horrible chapter in my life and studying others who passed or almost passed away, I found out more.

I learned a major lesson after the famous Celebrity Chef, Anthony Bourdain died tragically through suicide. One of his best friends came out and said: "Anthony would do anything for anyone. The only person he didn't care about was himself." You may or may not have ever felt this level of pain, but either way, there is a major life lesson in this. No matter how hard things get, you must show up for yourself. You owe you! That's why the first person you must add to your team is you. John C. Maxwell famously said: "Whenever I see a person beginning to separate themselves from the pack, it's almost always due to personal growth." Next, it's all about identifying who the rest of your team is comprised of. You might be asking yourself, how do I even start the process of building my team?

First, know who is involved. Your team is comprised of yourself, your employees and your business relationships. So start thinking about how many people are currently on your roster and how many more you can support. It's important that you don't create a never-ending list of people because there aren't enough hours in the day to serve and love that many people at the highest level. Aristotle once said, "a friend to all, is a friend to none".

Next, let's nail down the other side, which is the missions that are closest to your heart. Have fun with this discovery process because whether you realize it or not; the answers have most likely been in your subconscious for a good majority of your life. Now it's time to pull them from your mind and get to work on truly supporting them. Here's a little tip to guide you on discovering what organizations mean the most. Perhaps, you know the feeling of being a foster child and would love to contribute to an organization in that area. Note that down. Maybe it breaks your heart to know that certain children don't have a strong family structure or won't be getting any toys for the holidays. Note that down. Maybe you have a good understanding of depression, anxiety or other mental illnesses, so mental health is important to you. Note that down. Hate knowing that certain animals never got to make it to a loving family? Note down the possibility of supporting animal shelters or rescues. I could go on forever about all of the endless ways that you can support organizations, but hopefully, this gives you a good starting point on your brainstorming process. Keep in mind that you or one of your team members will be in direct touch with them for years to come (sort of like a partnership) so choose organizations that you want to support long-term.

"Whenever I see a person beginning to separate themselves from the pack, it's almost always due to personal growth."

John C. Maxwell

I can honestly tell you that when you're laser-focused on pouring into the people and missions that mean the most to you, your drive becomes unmatched. You're no longer the entrepreneur who says I'm in business to make as much money as possible and end it there.

Rather, with conviction, you stake your claim with confidence, and it sounds a little something like this. "Of course, I'm in business to make as much money as possible. Who isn't? But for me, being a business owner means much more. It also means that I can intentionally show up and give back to those who need it the most, including my team and my community."

TAKE ACTION:

1. Visit JonMajak.com/RingTheBell and download and fill out the "Build Your Perfect Customer Avatar" Worksheet.
2. Keep this worksheet handy. As we progress through the book, I'll teach you what growth engines you need to deploy to pummel your customer avatar with laser targeted marketing.

CHAPTER 5:
MINDSET IS EVERYTHING

By the grace of God and by pure adrenaline, you've made it to the top. You dust yourself off, stand upright and see the magnificent bell right in front of you. It's even more powerful and glorious than you could have ever imagined. You also can't help but notice the thriving town below. You were so focused on the climb that you never really noticed how busy the city was below. Your eyes begin to water, and emotions take over your body. That's when you catch yourself being taken over by the unknown, and your nerves start getting the best of you.

However, you're resilient and have a newly developed level of mental toughness. You realize that in order for you to swing that rope as hard as you could, you need to make sure your mindset and foundation is solid and you're rooted into the ground. So you dig your heels into the dirt-covered, jagged mountain-top and say a quick prayer. Something's telling you that once you ring that bell, life will never be the same- and you're right.

🔔

The moment has arrived. It's time to grip that rope and swing and smash it like it's nobody's business. The question remains, are you ready? If you have the right mindset, you are. Alexander Graham Bell once said: "Before anything else, preparation is the key to success." Your mindset must be all about preparedness, growth, and excellence at this stage.

In short, if you want to absolutely dominate the game, then you need to think differently. You need to think and operate like the pinnacle category in home service, and that is like HVAC companies

(Heating, Ventilation and Air Conditioning). Think about it for a minute. Which service companies do you traditionally see with a fleet of wrapped vehicles and big businesses? The 8 and 9-figure service companies typically play in the HVAC world. Seeing these monstrous companies thrive should open your eyes to what's possible. I can tell you this. The killer companies in this space hire and train like no other. Their SOPs, manuals and software are next-level. Their culture, admin, sales and marketing are on a different level. They have recurring revenue built into their model by embedding maintenance contracts into their system. So what can you learn from them? Everything! First, start by acknowledging that it all begins with the business owners' mindset.

"Before anything else, preparation is the key to success."
Alexander Graham Bell

For all of this to work out, you must have a business that can handle an influx of new leads and ensure everyone strives to operate at the level of excellence. In business terms, this means you absolutely must have your Organizational Chart built out and supported by clear roles and responsibilities. This way, when the new business floods in, the team doesn't fumble and throw their hands up in confusion but rather catches the ball and runs into the end zone by executing like a monster. Every single team member plays an important role at this moment. You are about to embark on the journey of a lifetime, but before you go too hard, remember this chapter.

Remember that your mindset must be in the right place. Remember that you must stop selling and start helping. If you can remember this quote from Richard Branson before you launch your growth engines, you will be operating from the right mental space. "Some entrepreneurs think; how can I make a lot of money? But the better way is to think, how can I make people's lives a lot better? If you get it right, the money will come." This is a book intended to turn your company into a money-generating machine, so it's only fitting to start with how to make as much money as possible.

This is where growth engines come in. Growth engines sound powerful because they really are! So what exactly is a growth engine? A growth engine involves any marketing activity that your company believes in suitable for your type of business. Some people use the terms marketing levers or lead generation sources, but that doesn't do it for me. When I'm marketing at a high level, I am looking to blow my damn socks off to the other side of the room with impact, and the only way to do that is with a loud and strong engine! Keep in mind that these marketing activities are deployed into your local market with one mission: to create massive growth.

This part is all about your mindset, so when you are building out your engines, remember that you aren't building a VW Bug engine. You are operating like a 9-figure HVAC owner and building a cigarette boat or Boeing airplane or, even further, a rocket ship. The end goal of growth engines is to ensure each activity is dialed in and firing hard. It will take a little bit of trial and error, but that's all part of the process.

The trial and error part is called your Testing Phase. This phase is all about imperfect action and seeing how the activity actually performs.

You run it for 60-90 days, tweak any areas of opportunity and gauge your ROI (Return on Investment). At a minimum, the ROI target should be 4 or 5-to-1 or greater. This means for every $1 you put in, you should be yielding $4 or $5 back in revenue minimum. I use this ROI gauge loosely because everyone wants a 5-to-1 return or greater. In fact, I want to see you have 10 to 1's or greater in due time, but I use 4 or 5 to 1 because that type of ROI generally supports scale.

Think about it for a minute. On a 2-to-1 basis, you are only doubling your money. That type of return simply doesn't support paying for your COGS (Cost of Goods Sold), payroll and investing back into the business. A helpful tip is to never test anything during off-season or when there is little demand for your service. For an effective test, you must test the marketing activity during the season or when demand is high. There is a simple yet powerful tool that must be used when analyzing your return on investment. It's called a Monthly Marketing Report. There are a bunch of complex ways to measure ROI per lead source but we can let the advanced CRMs get granular for you.

I'll show you how to easily create a basic one in Chapter 6.

Campfire Chat with Expert Mountain Climber:

Roland Ligtenberg, Co-founder of Housecall Pro

About Roland:

Roland Ligtenberg, Co-Founder and SVP of Growth and Innovation at Housecall Pro, is passionate about finding scalable growth channels through relentless zero-to-one execution. He loves creating product growth loops while simultaneously building out operationally & CAC-efficient sales and marketing teams.

Housecall Pro is revolutionizing the SMB home services industry through a SaaS-enabled marketplace & mobile operating system. In under 7 years, 100,000+ home service professionals use the platform on average 7+ hours a day to streamline and modernize their business through software & automation. 10+ billion dollars of home service work is transacted through the platform yearly. Previously, he was part of the founding team at Qualcomm Labs and, as a serial entrepreneur, built businesses in various industries like scuba diving, poker, house painting, and EDM music. In his free time, he enjoys sailing internationally, piloting his fleet of drones, operating his vineyard, and overlanding in his Jeep.

JM: Hey Roland! Thanks for joining me around the campfire, always a pleasure. I know you've put a ton of time and resources into making sure homeowners have the best experience possible. Why is delivering the best customer experience so important in today's day and age?

RL: In a world where everything is being commoditized, the one thing that will never be is the full customer experience. It's important to embrace tools like Housecall Pro that can help improve the customer experience digitally and set expectations before technicians even arrive. At the end of the day, people will remember how you made them feel, and that differentiation in a crowded market will make all the difference.

JM: In a highly competitive market, the lasting impression a business leaves on its customers is what truly sets it apart. What type of features do homeowners appreciate the most? Why?

RL: There's a huge list of features that homeowners love when a service professional uses Housecall Pro. The On My Way texts, pictures of technicians before arrival, ability to pay in a modern way (online pay or pay by text), integrated awkwardness-free homeowner financing, online booking + built-in web-chat and more. All of these features help by increasing transparency during service and also allowing homeowners to pay in the way that they can afford. Remember, less than half of U.S. households — about 4 in 10 — are able to cover an unexpected $1,000 expense like a car or home repair or medical bill.

JM: This is really insightful information, Roland! Why is it important for home service providers to know who their customer avatar is? What are some tips on defining their avatar?

RL: A mistake commonly made by home service providers is that they either don't have customer personas at all or try to define just one.

There never is just one, and it's important to look at the data of your existing customer database in addition to defining other personas you would like to attract. A simple tip is to look inside your Housecall Pro account and sort by ZIP or by tags, then append that data with information from data.census.gov.

JM: That is a great tip, Roland. The next question I have revolves around leverage. How should home service providers be leveraging and attacking their day if they want to be the best in their local market?

RL: You should always think about what activities you can be doing daily that compound. A great example is making sure that every opportunity you get you are delivering more value than you're getting paid for, asking for customer referrals and reviews on every job, and making sure the customers' neighbors know you were in the area and are the local company to call if they need your help.

JM: Love it! Going above and beyond will make you stand out from the rest for sure. Lastly, What advice do you have for anyone who is currently climbing their own mountain?

RL: In every decision you face, think about the short-term and long-term consequences. People most often act based on avoiding short-term pain because that is what we do as humans. Oftentimes it's the wrong decision, and it's those that can endure short-term pain, discomfort, feeling like a fool, that end up making the decisions for the long-term. It's okay to descend from the mountain, even if you're 3/4 of the way there, to start anew at the bottom and carve and try a new path.

🔔

The next phase comes after your initial 60-90 day test, and it's called your Ongoing Optimization Phase. This phase simply means that once it passes the test, you keep your eye on the ball and continue to work towards enhancing your ROI as you progress. This is where traction picks up and the growth engine starts to really generate steam. There is no set time frame in this phase because it graduated through the strict testing phase and earned its spot as a permanent fixture. As a best practice, aim to optimize the activity to its peak performance and then advance it to a permanent system for your company moving forward.

For your point of reference, certain activities take much longer to optimize than others. Magazine ad copy can be tweaked monthly and will take longer than optimizing a Google Ad campaign which can happen in real-time. The Ongoing Optimization phase is all about having a mindset of "tweaking approaches and continuous improvement." Here are a handful of items to help you optimize in this phase. Optimizing tactics include but are certainly not limited to changing designs on your flyers, changing colors and font on your website, adding or removing keywords in your Google Ads campaign, revising your Text Blast message, tweaking your email creative and much more. Always remember, if something isn't working that doesn't mean that you should throw in the towel. It means you need to keep changing your approach until you've fully tested the engine and proceed accordingly.

I believe that every excellent business has a set standard of at least 10 growth engines that must be constant. Another 3 to 5 should be predictably coming in and out of your system throughout the year, depending on your marketing calendar. We'll dig into the importance of having a marketing calendar shortly. Some examples of growth engines in the home service business are Google Ads, Facebook Ads, SEO, Trade shows, Door Hangers, Yard Signs, Text Message Software and Email Marketing Software. It's crucial that you're aware that not all growth engines are created equal. Certain engines work much better in certain areas of the country than others. For example, I believe the Nextdoor App is a powerful engine if it's utilized in an area where recommendations are hot, and the App is used at a high level.

But I don't believe the Nextdoor App is valuable in a small town where there might not be much engagement. It would be an extremely ineffective use of your time and money to place it into the Ongoing Optimization Phase if this were the case. As long as you keep your finger on the pulse of what converts best in your local market, you are on the right track. Another good visual example is the growth engine of trade shows. Certain businesses just don't do well at conventions, home shows or property management expos, while others perform extremely well. It all comes down to your market and how your potential customers are responding. That's why we have 2 phases to our growth engines. Never discount a marketing activity until you have thoroughly tested it in Phase 1, The Testing Phase. For example, before you say Trade shows don't work in your market, you must look in the mirror and ask yourself a few hard questions such as the following.

Did I have an excellent booth display with excellent marketing collateral to support the effort? Did I have on catchy professional attire, and was my team super outgoing? Did we push out an excellent offer? Can we do better if our booth location was in a prime spot next time? Remember, keep the mindset of excellence during this discovery process, and it won't feel like work. Because the next time you attend a trade show, you'll be one step closer to being consistently excellent. Let's use another example, and this one will be for an online growth engine. Keep in mind, never discredit a marketing activity until you have tweaked your approach countless times and exhausted every option to optimize.

Let's say you're running Google Ads for 90 days, and you aren't seeing the ROI you were hoping for. Here are a few questions you should ask yourself before putting a halt to this activity. Did I have a healthy enough budget to compete in my market? Was my campaign dialed in enough with specific search terms that led to a corresponding page on my website? Do I have an excellent reputation in my market, or do I have a ton of unanswered 1-star Google Reviews? Could we have improved ways to increase our closing rate? Did we test this during our busy season and not during our off-season? I could go on for a while, but I hope this makes sense. Remove all of your emotions and be objective during this process. This is not a subjective process; it's black and white and very objective. In a nutshell, make sure to slam the throttle down on the activities that work and hit the brakes on the activities that aren't cutting the mustard.

Growth engines are the secret sauce to ringing the bell like crazy, but first you must have three fundamental items in place. I'm dropping this line here as a reminder - "Keep thinking like a 9-figure HVAC Owner!" These three items are your branding, website and online reputation. When they are on point, your growth engines hum a lot stronger and smoother.

The first component is your branding. Good businesses think of it as your logo but you operate at the standard of excellence so you know it's much more than that. Technically speaking, your branding includes your logo, tagline and mascot or caricature, font styles and more. I like to go a bit further and say branding is the feeling your company gives someone. The colors used must be designed to be super impactful and inviting. I suggest bright, vibrant colors that appeal to and welcome new prospects. Having a mascot or caricature isn't essential, but it is always a good idea if the name of your company could support one.

For example, check out my friend Tommy Mello's A1 Garage Doors brand. He is the master at driving forward brand congruence. His business cards, marketing collateral, website, signage and anything you can think of are all massively congruent. When your brand congruence is next level, you take the customer experience to the next level, and that means more and more sales will pour in.

When crafting your tagline, remember to keep it simple. No one wants to read a run-on sentence. Don't fall short here. If your brand is weak, your marketing will be weak. If your brand is a powerhouse, your marketing will follow suit. Once the brand comes together, have your graphic designer place all the assets into something called a brand manual or brand guideline manual. Brand manuals are documents that explain how a brand should be presented in public and how people should come into contact with it. They are used not only by those working within the company but also, most importantly, by those using the brand externally. Features include exact color codes, font styles and more. Once you have your brand created, it's time to protect your investment. This is when you know it's time to hire an experienced trademark attorney to make sure you filed and own any/all marks and copyrights. Powerful brands get mimicked and replicated every day, and you'll have nothing to stand on if you don't own the rights, so do not overlook this step.

Second, I can't stress the importance of having a powerful website. Most websites out there are built as informational brochures, which means they are simply leaving way too much money on the table. Your website should be thoughtfully crafted with user experience in mind. It needs to also be built as a lead machine. It should have large clickable phone numbers throughout the site as well as strategically placed contact forms. It's important that those contact forms do not have too many fields that are required for Mrs. Jones to fill out. I've always been a firm believer that a lead is only as good as the person who works it.

That's why you should only require your website visitors to fill out their name, email, phone number and the service that they are interested in. (This only applies if you aren't using automatic bidding software on your website.) When you require too many fields, you restrict the flow of your lead faucet too much. Open the faucet up and make sure you remember less is more. Then when your leads come in, you can ask discovery questions such as what their address is and where they heard about you etc. Your contact form is not the place to nail that down. Your website should also be bright, clean and offer an incredible user experience meaning it shouldn't be bombarded with text and appear overwhelming.

Your site should have excellent content, such as impactful text and visual images and videos. Your site should also exemplify trust on every level so make sure it has an area there that's all about video testimonials and Google reviews.

"The end goal of growth engines is to ensure each activity is dialed in and firing hard."

Jon Majak

Search behavior is always changing, and let's face it, we live in an untrustworthy world. So the more you can get ahead of these buyer concerns and earn their trust through real reviews and testimonials, the more likely you are to convert Mrs. Jones from a website visitor into a paying customer. You should have a gallery that shows before and after photos. There should be zero stock images on your website, and instead should be pictures of your uniformed team performing work in a safe manner. Again, this inspires trust and shows the website visitor that you are an excellent company that arrives professionally and takes their job very seriously.

You should always have a careers tab built into your website where potential employees can always apply. That careers page should showcase a fun culture-based sizzle video that exemplifies why your company is top-notch and why potential hires should consider joining your squad. It's very important that you have a "Giving Back" page on your website because when you ring the bell, you are all about making an impact and giving back as much as possible. This page should outline the organization or organizations you support, why you support them and how your potential customers can join the cause. Make sure your "About Us" page is personalized and tells your story. Customers truly enjoy storytelling, so take your time and make sure you're spoon-feeding them a message that they will enjoy.

To go a bit further, you should actually have individual pages for each city that you service. Perception is reality, and when Mrs. Jones clicks on the city page where she is located, she will decode the message as your business is a local service expert in her local market. Locality boosts trust and, once again, increases your conversion rate. I could go on for probably another five chapters about tactics to ensure your website is firing on all cylinders, but I'll wrap it up by saying ensure it's mobile-friendly. Over 60% of website traffic comes from mobile devices so make sure your site is fast, responsive and is optimized for mobile traffic.

Third, let's talk for a moment about the importance of reviews and recommendations. Before I go on elaborating about how important these are, let me paint a picture for you so everything hits home.

Imagine yourself and your spouse going on a wonderful vacation out of town, where you know nothing or nobody. You are starting from square one and don't know any streets, highways, local bars or restaurants, nightlife events or much of anything else. Say you were looking to have a really magical night because, after all, as a hard-working entrepreneur, you don't get out as much as you need to. So this vacation really matters.

As you start to think about where you are going to dinner, what do you do? This isn't a rhetorical question. What do you do when you are looking for the best restaurant to visit for your short stay to make sure you have an excellent experience? If you're anything like me, you are opening up Google, and you are doing a search for the places with the best reviews in the area. Then you are digging into those reviews to make sure they are real and hopefully even catching some images or videos to support your decision. Then depending on which ones you like the most, you will go ahead and choose the best place possible. That's exactly how your potential customers are searching for home service professionals! Some people have some good recommendations, and others have heard about a few great locations to visit, but for the good majority of us- we are doing our due diligence and finding a trusted place that we're positive will give us the best chance of an excellent experience. So it begs the question. If this is how you search and this is what your search behavior looks like, are you doing everything possible to make sure your small business is showing up during moments like this?

So here we are in one of the craziest times in human history, and it's safe to say that, unfortunately, the world is at odds with each other in many ways. This also means that there is a lack of trust out there. It's your job as a high-level entrepreneur to see this as an advantage and not a disadvantage. Remember, your mindset is different from others. Use this growth mindset to build and earn trust at every angle. That's exactly why you need to have a lot of reviews and an active review generation system pumping every single day. You know that consumer search behavior is constantly changing. The way we searched for home services 20 years ago was in a big yellow book filled with every business you could imagine. The only companies who stood out were the ones who forked over an arm and a leg for large print advertisements.

No one thought about cross-referencing reviews but rather kept their fingers crossed that the company showing up to their house would be a home run hitter. These days, it doesn't matter if you're being found through Google Ads, SEO, Thumbtack, Local Magazines, Door hangers, Yard signs or anywhere else. There's a very high chance that Mrs. Jones is cross-referencing her buying decision with your reputation. She'd be doing herself an injustice by not doing so. Anyone can advertise, but not everyone can build a powerhouse brand built on a solid reputation. Always make sure your target is the ladder. I'm a big believer in making sure you do not depend on one major review source, either.

All things considered, I will always push for the importance of Google reviews. That should not be the only place you drive and generate recommendations and reviews, though. Do your best to build a reputation on every single social platform where your customer avatar lives and breathes. LinkedIn recommendations matter when you do a lot of commercial business. Facebook definitely matters in your local market because most of your customers have a Facebook profile and are active on it. Neighborhood apps matter because they're a local, trusted source in your community. Do your best to shine bright in there if this is a pond you fish from. When it's all said and done, more reviews equals more revenue.

It's very important that you have automation set up in your business to attain these review targets as well. For example, there are review generation platforms out there that will send an automatic text message to the customer the minute that their credit card is processed in QuickBooks. It's called a post-transaction review request, and if it's done right, it will skyrocket your review generation process. You can also have a system in place where your technicians are responsible for gaining reviews. This is how we drew over 500 Google reviews very fast.

Here's a brief overview of what my Review Generation system looked like in my previous home service business. Our technicians would arrive at the job site, knock on the door to greet Mrs. Jones and then explain how our process worked. Then they would let them know that they had one main goal in mind. That was to do the very best job possible in the most efficient manner so they could ultimately earn a five-star review and turn them into a customer for life. Our technicians were actually trained to build rapport when they arrived and then directly tell the customer that they were going to ask for a five-star review before they left the property if they did a great job. Then they would get the customer to agree to those unthreatening terms in a friendly manner.

Once the job was wrapped up, our lead technician would knock on the door and ask Mrs. Jones to do a walk around on site to make sure she was thrilled with the service and that she signed off on a job well done. Then the technician would say: "As promised, I made sure to clean your property as if it were my own. Is it safe to say that we earned that five-star review from you today?" It never fails, and it never will. The reason is that they set clear expectations and delivered. Next, the technician would send the review request directly to Mrs. Jones from his mobile phone and ask if she could fill it out as before we departed the property. (A helpful reminder is to always push urgency as it really drives conversions.) The software then sent a text message and went after the review conversion. If Mrs. Jones wasn't able to knock out the review in a timely manner, the software would re-initiate another request through text message and/or email over the next day or two.

Eventually, the review gets filled out, and you're off to apply the same system at the next job. There really is no scientific formula to be a beast at review generation. In fact, some high-level entrepreneurs don't have their technicians go in for the request and have their sales staff go after it. Other companies have their administrative team follow up on the job and ask how the service was, and then ask for a review. There are several ways to skin a cat. You must do what is best for you and your organization. Do not reinvent the wheel; make sure you put something in place where your team can be financially incentivized, and it enhances the experience for both your technicians and the customer when it's all said and done. When you and your team operate in the mindset of excellence, aka the 9-figure HVAC company, day in and day out, your business will naturally explode!

TAKE ACTION:

1. Do you have a fixed mindset or a growth mindset? If fixed, how do you plan on changing this to growth? If growth, why?
2. Post your answer on social media with the hashtags #mindset #ringthebell

CHAPTER 6:
HOW YOU RING IT FOR MONEY

T*he big moment has arrived. You grip the rope tightly and ring the bell as hard as you possibly can, over and over again. It's so loud, but you block out the sound, and for some reason, you can't even stop. You're ringing it so hard, and you notice people coming out of their homes and businesses to see what all the noise is about.*

In these homes and businesses, people can't help but open their front doors and stare at the top of the mountain. They are rolling down their car windows, and some people are even jumping out to catch a glimpse of the man creating the loudest sound anyone has ever heard in town.

🔔

I must preface this chapter by mentioning that anyone can operate at a 'fair to good' level and get some of these growth engines moving. I say this because I know if you are reading this book, you aren't looking to build an average business. You are looking to build an excellent business on every level. Excellent businesses don't wing things, they build and execute on proven systems. What's a system? A system is a documented procedure that outlines how to do something in your organization to achieve your business goals. Every single growth engine you have in place, must be supported by a documented system that your team must follow in order to achieve excellence. As I coach some of the hungriest entrepreneurs I've ever come across, I drill down system implementation like no other. The reason being is that systems remove chaos in a business. They add clarity, and if you build a system-dependent business, instead of a people-dependent business, your company is set to scale. It doesn't matter if it's a marketing system, production system or anything in between; the right system will propel a small business to the next level quickly. Be mindful of how much you should be allocating as part of your marketing budget as well. I don't want you spending with no cap in mind and looking at advertising as a simple expense. I advise that you look at it as an investment and strategically spend anywhere from 3 to 8% of your total sales on marketing. That means, if you are doing $1,000,000 in sales, it's perfectly acceptable to allocate $30,000 to $80,000 to your advertising budget, depending on how hard you want to go. As a reference, some companies spend more than this if they are in full blown growth mode while others spend less and only grow organically.

"Every single growth engine you have in place, must be supported by a documented system in order to achieve excellence."

Jon Majak

To ensure you execute this in the easiest way possible, I'm first going to list, define and explain every growth engine (marketing activity) you should have on your radar. I'm sliding in a handful of sales growth engines in this as well. Why? Because they have a strong marketing component embedded into them, and I don't want you to leave these out as your drive forward. There are certain engines that I am leaving out on purpose, because they are simply a waste of time and energy. This book is not about fluff, it's about opening your eyes to every single activity I've personally seen and can vouch for that works in the home service vertical. Remember, what works for some businesses, doesn't work for others. The only way you will know what's vital in your local market is to become a testing and executing machine. Get through the dirty work of testing and hit the gas on the engines that matter most. When (not if) you do this right, you will experience explosive growth. Don't say I didn't warn you!

 Ring the Bell Bonus

Visit JonMajak.com/RingtheBell and download the "Ring the Bell for Money- Growth Engine Document System." All you have to do is fill out each page and set it in motion.

ONLINE GROWTH ENGINES

Marketing activities that are performed digitally

Growth Engines that are Absolute Musts
(Primary Lead Sources)

Google Ads:

Google Ads is an online advertising platform developed by Google, where advertisers bid to display brief advertisements, service offerings, product listings, or videos to web users.

Primary mission: Obtain New Business

How you will make the most money from it: There are levels to this answer. First, get Search Ads up immediately. Next, integrate Display Ads (Geared more to Brand Awareness) if the budget permits. Third, get a video made and have it showcased on YouTube if the budget permits. Label this as your Google Ads System. Test out what works best for your company, document the system and set it in motion.

Local Services Ads (aka Google Guaranteed):

Local Services Ads help you connect with people who search on Google for the services you offer. Your ads will show up for customers in your area, and you only pay if a customer contacts you directly through the ad. It's also known as Google Guaranteed and is gaining in popularity as the years go on. It's not available for every industry quite yet, but I'd imagine it will be in time.

Primary mission: Obtain New Business

How you will make the most money from it: If LSAs are available in your market, get on it. They are powerful because they are often displayed at the top of the search engine with a green Google Guaranteed Checkmark. It's a fairly simple process; build out your profile and make sure you select the correct categories for your business to receive leads for. The model is on a cost per lead basis, so you can turn it on and off with the click of a button. Label this as your Google LSA System. Test out what works best for your company, document the system and set it in motion.

Search Engine Optimization:

Search Engine Optimization is the process of improving the quality and quantity of website traffic to a website from search engines. SEO targets unpaid traffic unlike paying per click like Google Ads. SEO is all about your organic rankings and making sure you are dominating on page 1 for the keywords or search terms that really matter for your business. There are several reasons why organic SEO matters. The first reason is whoever owns the most market-share on page 1 of Google typically smokes their competition (Pardon the shameless Mr. Pipeline reference.) Think about it, if you have Google Ads getting you on page 1 and then your SEO efforts land you another 2 spots on Google, you have much more visibility than your competition. Another benefit of SEO is that when you appear on page 1 organically, you appear more trusted and established which historically leads to high ticket projects. One of the most underrated reasons why you should put great effort into organic rankings comes from my personal experience. I'll never forget sitting at the table when I was selling one of my service businesses.

The gentleman who bought my business looked at me and said, "I like your vehicles, but I already have strong vehicles. I like your employees, but I have strong employees too. What I really want are your page 1 rankings and your online presence. He wanted my digital assets. All of that time I invested into making sure we dominated in our market finally paid off. Well, it paid off through all of the business we took in, but it was really exciting when somebody said it would take so many years to achieve that type of success online, and I really want that. There's no doubt SEO boosts the worth of your business. Never sleep on valuation. Another great reason why you should focus on this area is that it will lower your customer acquisition costs over time. This allows you to not rely on Google Ads forever. One thing to take note of is people's search behavior. So remember, when crafting your website and SEO strategy, think about how people voice search. (Ex: Hey Siri, show me HVAC companies near me.) The right SEO team will make sure you are ahead of the curve on this strategy.

Primary mission: Increase visibility and local dominance

How you will make the most money from it: SEO is crucial but should never be your primary lead source. Don't do SEO unless you have constant leads flowing in and you have a budget to invest in. SEO results can take anywhere from 6-12 months to see real traction take place. If the budget permits, invest ASAP. Rank locally for all the "money keywords" that matter for your business. Label this your SEO System. Test out what works best for your company, document the system and set it in motion.

Google Business Profile:

As the name implies, Google Business Profile is a free service and it allows you to create a business listing on Google. It ensures you provide the necessary information customers need to visit your office, contact your company or make a purchase. GBP is also necessary for SEO, and it houses your Google Reviews, so this is an absolute must. It also showcases your service area, business hours of operation, and other relevant business information. It's also another way for your customers to connect and interact with you.

Primary mission: Increase visibility and local dominance

How you will make the most money from it: You need to take on the mission of shining the brightest in your market. That means that you need more Google Reviews (and Owner Responses), Consistent Images & Videos Added Weekly, Relevant Search Terms in your profile and ultimately, make sure you're optimizing it often. Label this as your Google Business Profile System. Test out what works best for your company, document the system and set it in motion.

Pro Tip: Get customers to leave reviews using some of your important keywords and service locations. I'm not saying this is a proven hack that works 100% of the time, but when you own a digital marketing agency and have a good look at the data behind the curtain on companies 'GBPs, I advise you consider doing this. For example: "We used ABC Service Company for our residential window cleaning in Miami, FL. They were prompt, caring and professional across the board. Highly recommend!"

Local Citations:

A local citation is any online mention of the **name, address, and phone number** of a local business. Citations can occur on local business directories, on websites, apps, and on social platforms. They help internet users discover local businesses and can also impact local search engine rankings. Specifically, having the right basic citations can help you rank accurately across all search engines. Local businesses can actively manage many citations to ensure data accuracy. Make sure your NAP (Name, Address, Phone Number) is consistent everywhere!

Primary mission: Increase visibility and local dominance

How you will make the most money from it: Take on the objective of increasing your visibility whenever you have the chance. Consumers often stumble into and visit these websites, so it's important you get on them. Call this your Local Citation System. Test out what works best for your company, document the system and set it in motion.

Bing Places for Business:

Bing Places for Business is a free service where you can manage your business listing on Bing Search and Maps. It's similar to Google Business Profile, but it's for the Bing platform. You can add the latest photos of your business and update your store hours. Do not discount the importance of being on Bing. Microsoft phones come with Bing preinstalled, and it's the default search engine on these phones. Bing is the second largest search engine in the world and has over 1 billion unique global visitors per month.

Primary mission: Increase visibility and local dominance

How you will make the most money from it: Get on this

platform as soon as possible. Fill it out as you would a Google Business Profile. It is another way to boost your online exposure and increase your online visibility. Call this your Bing for Places System. Test out what works best for your company, document the system and set it in motion.

Apple Maps:

Similar to Google Business Profile, the Apple Maps Connect portal serves as the home base for claiming businesses on Apple Maps. Apple Maps listings provide the opportunity for small business owners to get in front of Apple users. These users can find business information, such as the place name, business category, and whether the business accepts Apple Pay or not. If you have a small business, you can use Apple Maps Connect to add or update your business information that's shown in Maps, to help customers find you.

Primary mission: Increase visibility and local dominance

How you will make the most money from it: Make sure you have an accurate listing here. Apple is dominating in so many areas, and they really have their eye on helping small businesses grow. Call this your Apple Maps System. Test out what works best for your company, document the system and set it in motion.

Facebook Ads:

Facebook Ads can help a business get much more visibility and engagement on Facebook. Whether you are seeking to generate leads or increase brand visibility, Facebook Ads offers a great reach for a fairly inexpensive rate compared to Google Ads. Facebook Ads can help to achieve a ton of impressions and even be set up to retarget people who fell off your website.

Primary mission: Obtain New Business

How you will make the most money from it: First, I'd test running Lead Generation Ads to see if it's worth it for your business. If that model does yield the ROI you need, then try a campaign that has the objective of receiving messages from prospects. Direct Messaging (DM'ing) a company is less threatening and historically opens up lead flow if the ad is built right. Plus, it's unconventional, and being different should intentionally be a part of your game-plan. Remember, you must seek a 4 or 5 to 1 ROI or greater. On top of it all, I highly recommend getting Retargeting Ads set up. These are the ads that show up after one of your website visitors browses your site and bounces off. Candidly, these are my favorite and a must, in my opinion. Side-note: you can create and run ads that showcase on Instagram in the Meta Business Suite Portal. Call this your Facebook Ads System. Test out what works best for your company, document the system and set it in motion.

Facebook:

Facebook's organic reach is a measure of the number of people who see your content on the social platform when you don't pay to boost that content. Essentially, it's everything involved in the Facebook platform minus the Ads component. To me, the value of Facebook for Home Service Businesses is fairly simple. Posting "Stories" or "Reels" shows your followers you are relevant, and it helps keep their eyes on you. Your business page should be a place to push out engaging content to your followers. Groups offer specific audiences, and if you leverage them correctly, you can make a killing by monetizing them. I call this "Fishing from Ponds." Consider direct messaging prospects and other companies that you can network and make money with an introduction as well. This is called Cold Direct Messaging and is super effective if done right.

Primary mission: Obtain New Business, Engage Customer-base and Build Relationships

How you will make the most money from it: Think about being "Top of Mind" every chance you get. The person and/or company that's seen the most, typically makes the most money. Do everything with the mindset of building real value and driving engagement. Some proven ways to generate leads are being involved in neighborhood groups, posting content to your feed and story as well as running contests or free giveaway raffles. Also, consider starting a local Facebook group for your neighborhood or city. An example of this is: "Moms of Miami" or "Miami Homeowner Talk." Post and build an audience, then tastefully post your services once the group is humming. Fishing from your own pond is fun. Call this your Facebook System. Test out what works best for your company, document the system and set it in motion.

Pro Tip: Hire a Virtual Assistant to cold DM prospects with template messages on a weekly basis. The message could look like this: **"Good morning Paul, my name is Sarah from ABC Service Company. How are you doing today?"** It's unthreatening, warm, and leaves the door open for a response by not having too many words. Have the VA DM every person in the ponds you want to fish from, every business you can make money with and every commercial prospect in town. This is a numbers game, and all it takes is one whale to bite to turn you into a believer.

Instagram:

Instagram is an entirely visual platform. Unlike Facebook, which relies on both text and pictures, Instagram's sole purpose is to enable users to share images or videos with their audience. Over 2 billion people use Instagram monthly, and 500 million of those users are on Instagram daily. Facebook aka Meta, owns Instagram, and the user base grows every day. I wouldn't suggest making Instagram your primary traffic source, but jobs will come from it if you are active enough. Post to your Feed, Stories and don't forget about Reels. Reels have an incredible reach!

Primary mission: Obtain New Business & Widen Your Audience

How you will make the most money from it: Post image and video oriented content as often as possible. Build out your followers and spoon-feed them value-added information. Consider making Instagram your place to also house and showcase everything culture related. Office events, outings and birthday celebrations make for great photos, and that's what Instagram is all about. The more you post culture-related content, the more you increase your trust and engagement with current and potential customers. Call this your Instagram System. Test out what works best for your company, document the system and set it in motion.

LinkedIn:

LinkedIn is the world's largest professional network on the internet. You can use LinkedIn to find the right job or internship, connect and strengthen professional relationships, and learn the skills you need to succeed in your career. Essentially, it's a great resource to find great talent and also a place to build out your network. It's a really good tool in the home service business to create and build professional relationships with hard-to-reach contacts such as property managers and likeminded business owners. There are over 800 million members and growing, so there's a ton of room to make things happen.

Primary mission: Obtain New Business & Build Relationships

How you will make the most money from it: Put on your networking hat and plant seeds with anyone you can make money with. Direct message an introduction to your competitors, vendors, other home service companies, property managers and much more. Call this your LinkedIn System. Test out what works best for your company, document the system and set it in motion.

YouTube:

YouTube is an online video-sharing and social media platform owned by Google. I've always had a feeling in my gut that YouTube's end goal is to replace television. I could be wrong, but either way, they have a massive audience. YouTube has more than 2.6 billion active users. More than a quarter of the world's population uses YouTube every month. Around half of internet users around the world have access to YouTube.

Primary mission: Obtain New Business and Increase visibility

How you will make the most money from it: You can make money on YouTube in a few ways. The first way is to create SEO-based videos that allow your company to be showcased on page 1 of Google. For example, create a video called "Condominium Gutter Installation" or "Hotel Window Cleaning Done Right." And support it with a great video of you doing so, and you might just leapfrog your competitors in the search engine. Lots of people will view this video, and in time, your perfect customer will too. Second, you can run ads and have your video displayed before other videos people are looking to watch. If you create a large and loyal following with a ton of viewership, YouTube will actually pay you on a residual basis. Call this your YouTube System. Test out what works best for your company, document the system and set it in motion.

Neighborhood Apps:

The Nextdoor App is a perfect example of a Neighborhood App. It's essentially a social platform that connects neighbors based on their location. They allow neighbors within the same geographical area to share information and communicate. This is a powerful platform because the Nextdoor App has over 66 million active users. 33 million of these users are active and trust me when I tell you, you want to be on their good side. That tells you there is a real demand for a localized community platform.

Primary mission: Obtain New Business and Gain Referrals

How you will make the most money from it: Here's a good place to start. Create a business page and then ask some of your loyal, long-time customers to post a quick recommendation of your business on the app. This will surely generate you some leads. Second, build out your Nextdoor Marketing System. For example, every time someone calls you and tells you that they found you on one of these apps, thank them for the opportunity earned and then do the following. As you close out the work order, do not ask for a Google review, ask Mrs. Jones if she would be kind enough to write a great recommendation on the app where she found you. Let her know how much it would mean to you and your small business. Be transparent and let her know that the more traction you gain on local apps like that, the more it will help your company get recognized and grow. Call this your Neighborhood App System. Test out what works best for your company, document the system and set it in motion.

Digital Marketing Agency:

In order to scale like crazy, you shouldn't be micromanaging every single digital marketing activity long-term. I always suggest being super present during testing to ensure everything is dialed in. You either need an internal team or a high-level marketing agency to handle this as your business grows. The right team or agency will be able to generate constant leads and help with any issues or concerns that inevitably pop up from time to time.

Primary mission: Obtain New Business & Increase Visibility

How you will make the most money from it: Digital marketing agencies have become a cornerstone for home service providers in the US. The best-in-class companies will help you generate leads, rank organically, boost your social presence and manage your website. If you aren't handling your online presence in-house, I recommend hiring a top provider as you grow your business. Call this your Marketing Agency System. Test out what works best for your company, document the system and set it in motion.

Growth Engines designed to add fuel to the fire
(Secondary Lead Sources)

Microsoft Advertising:

Microsoft Advertising is a service that provides pay-per-click advertising on the Bing, Yahoo!, and DuckDuckGo search engines. Microsoft Ads can be more cost-effective than Google Ads because of its cheaper CPC (cost-per-click). There is much less competition on this platform. Figures vary, but CPCs can be anywhere from 32.5% to 60.2% less than Google Ads.

Primary mission: Obtain New Business

How you will make the most money from it: Get ads up on Microsoft Advertising if you want to reach a wider audience. It's worth it from my experience, because the costs per click are so inexpensive. It opens up the faucet for lead flow because people are searching on Bing, Yahoo and DuckDuckGo every day. Label this as your Microsoft Ads System. Test out what works best for your company, document the system and set it in motion.

TikTok:

TikTok is a social media platform for creating, sharing and discovering short videos. The app is primarily used by young people as an outlet to express themselves through singing, dancing, and comedy, and it allows users to create videos and share them across a community. This platform is evolving daily and becoming more and more relevant for adults and business owners. There are currently 1.5 billion users of which 1 billion are active monthly.

Primary mission: Grow your influence & widen your audience

How you will make the most money from it: You can monetize this creative platform in a few ways. First, you can build such a loyal and growing follower base that TikTok will actually compensate you for your efforts. Second, if you get in front of the right customers, they will buy from you. I wouldn't make it a primary place to generate leads, but I would certainly make sure I post on it often to easily grow my influence and boost my online visibility. Call this your TikTok System. Test out what works best for your company, document the system and set it in motion.

Neighborhood Websites:

Some neighborhoods have their own websites that show information on HOA rules, paint colors schemes, events in the neighborhood, etc. These websites are important because your perfect customer is most likely putting their eyes on it at some point. They don't get a massive amount of web traffic, but the people who visit neighborhood websites are typically solid customers. Traditionally, they are seeking licensed, insured companies that come highly recommended by the higher-ups in the neighborhood.

Primary mission: Obtain New Business

How you will make the most money from it: Create a list of every single neighborhood in your service area. The list should be extensive and thorough. Then do your diligence and start turning over every stone to see if these neighborhoods have websites. If they do, call them and see what it would take to advertise or get a banner up. Consider bartering in this situation. Call this your Neighborhood Website System. Test out what works best for your company, document the system and set it in motion.

Reddit:

Reddit is a social news website and forum where content is socially curated and promoted by site members through voting. The site name is a play on the words "I read it." Reddit member registration is free, and it is required to use the website's basic features.

Primary mission: Increase visibility and generate new business

How you will make the most money from it: Create a free account and make sure you don't spam the site at all. Think about serving the community at every turn. A good start is to search r/CityName (ex: r/Miami) then search within the subreddit for the service you offer (ex: Roofing) There are so many homeowners seeking the service you offer and truly value the advice from the trusted Reddit community. Another tip is to post in your city subreddit on a weekly basis about something generic that ties back to your business such as weather updates and how homeowners can prepare accordingly. Call this your Reddit System. Test out what works best for your company, document the system and set it in motion.

Yelp:

Yelp's website, Yelp.com, is a crowd-sourced local business review and social networking site. The site has pages devoted to individual locations, such as restaurants or service companies, where Yelp users can submit a review of their products or services using a one-to-five star rating scale.

Primary mission: Increase visibility and local dominance

How you will make the most money from it: Create a free listing on this platform. You will get link juice for being aligned with them and might even grab some leads. Like any platform, some companies excel on Yelp, while it might not be the best fit for others. Call this your Yelp System. Test out what works best for your company, document the system and set it in motion.

X (formerly Twitter):

X is a service for friends, family, and coworkers to communicate and stay connected through the exchange of quick, frequent messages. People post photos, videos, links, and text. These messages are posted to your profile, sent to your followers, and are searchable on search.

Primary mission: Increase visibility and local dominance

How you will make the most money from it: Create a free listing on this platform. You will get link juice for being aligned with this website. Post often and there will be a chance your profile might rank on page 1 of the search engine. It won't pour in the leads by any means but it will earn your company another piece of real estate on page 1 of the search engines. Call this your X System. Test out what works best for your company, document the system and set it in motion.

Lead Providers:

There are great lead providers that generate leads for Home Service companies all over the internet. Some generate them through their own websites like Angi, Craftjack and Thumbtack, while others generate them through email, cold calling and other strategic methods. If you plug into a credible lead provider, they will consistently send you quality leads. Lots of lead generation companies have a bad reputation so stay clear of anyone who sets your intuition on red alert.

Primary mission: Obtain New Business

How you will make the most money from it: Run small tests of $500 from each provider you have interest in. Large lead providers work very well in certain markets, while smaller private lead generators work great in others. Green light any providers that get you a 4 to 5 times ROI or greater and hit the brakes on companies who wasted your time. Call this your Lead Provider System. Test out what works best for your company, document the system and set it in motion.

OFFLINE GROWTH ENGINES

Marketing activities that are done outside of the web

Growth Engines that are Absolute Musts
(Primary Lead Sources)

Vehicle Wraps:

A vehicle vinyl wrap describes the automotive aftermarket practice of completely or partially covering a vehicle's original paint with your branding information. It's a crucial piece to the puzzle of dominating your market and, if done correctly, will be a rolling billboard and lead-generating machine.

Primary mission: Obtain New Business & Enhance Professionalism

How you will make the most money from it: Invest in a wrap as soon as possible. Brace yourself, because it's not cheap, so make sure you find a good price that fits your budget. Make sure the wrap is bold, unique, and offers the "wow factor" that you need to stand out. Ensure you have your brand, service, website and phone number showcased loud and proud. Never forget, less text is often more, when it comes to wraps. Call this your Vehicle Wrap System. Test out what works best for your company, document the system and set it in motion.

Professional Uniforms:

Professional uniforms make a huge difference in business. They tell a story if you do it right. Your management feels more respectable.

Your office staff feels professional, and your technicians feel like experts and stand out like a dynamic billboard. Most importantly, your customers love professional uniforms. They want to know that they hired professionals, and it boosts trust significantly.

Primary mission: Obtain New Business & Enhance Professionalism

How you will make the most money from it: Ensure that the uniforms are simple yet impactful. Remember, what your leadership team and office staff wear will most likely be different than your technicians. The first will be more collared shirts, while the second will be much bolder and friendlier for technicians. For technicians, make sure the shirts are vibrant and include a readable website address and a bold phone number. Techs go everywhere in these shirts from gas stations to restaurants and many other places between servicing customers. Take advantage of the visibility and make sure the shirts are created to generate more leads. Call this your Uniform System. Test out what works best for your company, document the system and set it in motion.

Conventions:

A convention or trade show is an event held to bring together members of a particular industry to display, demonstrate, and discuss their latest products and services. They are essential to any business's growth and carry a vast amount of benefits.

Primary mission: Obtain New Business & Networking

How you will make the most money from it: Do not blend in at all. Anyone can have a standard booth with some marketing materials. Make sure your booth stands out and is super professional. Your collateral must be on point and something people actually use. Don't forget about ensuring your team is uniformed and dressed in something that stands out. Most importantly, have a game plan and execute on it. Don't just set up a basic booth, sit down timid and wait for people to approach you. Instead, get a list of vendors and attendees prior to the show and connect with them. Book meetings with the people you want to grow your relationships with (vendors, competitors, suppliers, etc.) and fill your schedule. Have a pitch down for when people are 5 feet away from your booth or closer. Be a networking machine and grow your business like crazy. Don't be afraid to have a great giveaway contest. People love free stuff so give away the chance to win something cool in return for a contact card dropped in your fishbowl. Call this your Convention System. Test out what works best for your company, document the system and set it in motion.

Pro Tip: A lead is only as good as the person who works it. Call and email every contact when you return from the show. You planted the seed when you met, now start the tilling proces of building the relationship. Eventually the seeds that matter will sprout. When you increase your network, you increase your net worth.

Cold Calling:

Cold calling is a technique in which a salesperson contacts individuals or businesses who have not previously expressed interest in your services.

Primary mission: Obtain New Business & Reach New Potential Customers

How you will make the most money from it: Focus on helping people, not selling people. Have authentic conversations, discover their pain points and offer a solution to fix their pain if they have one. As my friend, Brandon Vaughn says, be a farmer, not a hunter. Become an expert at planting as many seeds as possible. Then, work towards watering the seed and tilling the soil (aka nurturing the lead). Eventually, the seeds start to sprout like crazy and so does your revenue! It's a numbers game so move with efficiency. Call this your Cold Calling System. Test out what works best for your company, document the system and set it in motion.

Unsolicited Bids:

An unsolicited bid is a proposal telling the prospect how you can help or service their property for a fee.

Primary mission: Obtain New Business

How you will make the most money from it: Hire a Virtual Assistant to gather a list of all the HOA's, Commercial Properties, Hotels, Motels, Government facilities, etc. Then have your VA connect with as many people as possible, offering them complimentary estimates to earn their business. This is another scenario where being an expert farmer is so important. Don't think about going in for the kill on this strategy but rather plant seeds and create value. Call this your Unsolicited Bids System. Test out what works best for your company, document the system and set it in motion.

Door Hangers:

A door hanger is a small flyer, generally rectangular in shape, cut to hang from the handle or knob of a door. They are often used to distribute print advertising to residential homes.

Primary mission: Obtain New Business

How you will make the most money from it: You need to build out a door hanger system and execute on it. Don't go into canvassing by just hanging these at random homes when you have time. Rather, know that you must go through 10-25k a month, and you hang them in every single neighborhood you work in. Know that you have a dedicated canvasser that passes them out one day a week and that your technicians pass out 5 door hangers, post job at every property they service. Set up your door hangers to auto replenish and be delivered every 90 days at your front door. Your system will do the work for you. Call this your Door Hanger System. Test out what works best for your company, document the system and set it in motion.

Clip Flyers:

Clip Flyers are a powerful way to spread the word fast. They are flyers with plastic clips binding the two edges together. This form of advertising is attractive because it's inexpensive to produce, and with the right amount of planning, you can distribute your flyers directly to your perfect customer's home in volume.

Primary mission: Obtain New Business

How you will make the most money from it: You guessed it! By building out a Clip Flyer System. Listing down which neighborhoods in your service area need to get them and how often they get delivered. Know the flyer that converts best and where to find the most inexpensive clips. Having a dedicated flyer distributor helps a lot too. Call this your Clip Flyer System. Test out what works best for your company, document the system and set it in motion.

Yard Signs:

Yard signs are small advertising signs that can be placed strategically on the streets, in neighborhoods and many other places to gain exposure and generate leads. Most are weather resistant, durable and another great way to make the phone ring!

Primary mission: Obtain New Business

How you will make the most money from it: Your yard sign system should be on fire. Start with your sales efforts. If you close jobs out in the field, consider adding a "coming soon" yard sign to the home you will be servicing. When you are servicing a property, place a sign that says "another beautiful job in progress" during service. If your customer is okay with leaving one out after the job is complete, leave out the "another beautiful property serviced" sign. Get creative with your system and don't overthink it. When it comes to design, keep it simple and bold. List a service, a call to action and a large phone number. Call this your Yard Sign System. Test out what works best for your company, document the system and set it in motion.

Gift Cards:

A gift card is a prepaid stored-value money card, usually issued by a home service provider, to be used as an alternative to cash for purchases within a particular time frame. These are super beneficial when building out your referral system.

Primary mission: Obtain Referrals

How you will make the most money from it: Give a couple gift cards to each customer after you service their property. Tell them that one is for their next service and the other is to give to a family member, friend or neighbor. Also, consider your commercial efforts with gift cards as well. Give 50 to every realtor you know and work for. Give some to similar businesses in a different industry and see if they can spread the good word. If you hand out 10 cards to every service business you come across, you will soon have business coming in from every angle. Call this your Gift Card System. Test out what works best for your company, document the system and set it in motion.

Business Cards:

Business cards are cards showcasing business information about a company and/or individual. They are shared during formal introductions as a convenience and a memory aid.

Primary mission: Obtain New Business & Enhance Professionalism

How you will make the most money from it: Pass them out every chance you get. Keep some in your office, wallet, your vehicle(s), your spouse's vehicle, golf bag, gym bag, suitcase and every other place you run into people. You never really know the next time you might meet a whale and wish you had a card. Call this your Business Card System. Test out what works best for your company, document the system and set it in motion.

Digital Business Card:

Virtual business cards function by scanning an image like a QR code or by emailing, or texting someone the custom URL. These are stored on your cell phone, display your contact information and really offer an innovative first impression.

Primary mission: Obtain New Business & Networking

How you will make the most money from it: Get your virtual contact card into as many phones as possible. It offers a real wow factor, and the person will never have the excuse they didn't have your number saved. They are a must for conventions and events. Call this your Digital Business Card System. Test out what works best for your company, document the system and set it in motion.

Commercial Marketing Collateral:

If you want to scale hard and fast, you must always be prepared to take on more commercial work. In this case, you must always have your commercial marketing collateral ready to go. I recommend a professionally branded folder with custom inserts inside. Inserts should include About Us, Why Choose Us for your Commercial Property, Our Testimonials, 'Before & After' pictures and Safety First (this includes your license and insurance info)

Primary mission: Obtain New Business

How you will make the most money from it: The best way is to set weekly and monthly KPIs that ensure your team is getting these folders into the right hands. These places should be all commercial based, such as restaurants, stadiums, hotels, shopping centers, schools, etc. Call this your Commercial Marketing Collateral System. Test out what works best for your company, document the system and set it in motion.

Niche Marketing Collateral:

Always keep in mind that you should tailor your collateral to the specific partner. This means if you are looking to work with more painters, then you should have marketing collateral that you give just to painters. The best part is, you just need to swap out one insert. These folders should include the exact same inserts as your commercial marketing collateral but just swap your 'Why Choose Us for your Commercial Needs' with the 'Why Painters Love Working with Us' insert. This page just talks their lingo and offers the value you provide. The same goes for Realtors, HOAs, Suppliers, etc.

Primary mission: Obtain Referrals

How you will make the most money from it: Get these folders out as often as possible. Set KPIs that ensure these custom pieces of literature are distributed on a weekly and monthly basis. Call this your Niche Marketing Collateral System. Test out what works best for your company, document the system and set it in motion.

Referral Partners:

Nothing beats a great referral program where someone is already warmed up or has closed the deal for you. When you have referral partners in place, you have built-in sales people spreading the word about your business like wildfire.

Primary mission: Obtain Referrals

How you will make the most money from it: The name of the game here is incentivizing. Offer a referral fee or kickback for every referred person that you close. This is reciprocal, and you can refer companies out for a referral fee or "cut" as well. Call this your Referral Partner System. Test out what works best for your company, document the system and set it in motion.

Commercial Prospecting Demos:

The demo model only works for some of the trades. For example, this is a powerful tactic in the exterior cleaning industry if you are looking to scale the commercial end of your business. The premise is to force your foot in the door and build relationships with commercial properties by offering a complimentary demonstration. This offers a "no obligation" experience to potential heavy hitters to see your professionalism, equipment and timeliness. If done right, you will close a ton of new business.

Primary mission: Obtain New Business

How you will make the most money from it: Here's an example but apply it to your industry and type of commercial property. Call restaurants and ask to speak with the manager. Tell them you are going to be in their area over the next couple of days and would love to meet them and offer a free demo of how your service works. Call ahead, be on time, be professional and build rapport. Over deliver and you'll land the project! Call this your Commercial Prospecting Demo System. Test out what works best for your company, document the system and set it in motion.

Accolades:

Awards and accolades can boost your organization's reputation, setting you "apart from the crowd." They cement your credibility and offer the perception of a trusted company in the community.

Primary mission: Obtain New Business & Boost Credibility

How you will make the most money from it: You can spread the recognition all over social media, which will lead to more exposure. You can embed the digital winner badge on your website and email signature for ongoing exposure. You can also display the recognition on marketing collateral and at events. Call this your Accolades System. Test out what works best for your company, document the system and set it in motion.

Campfire Chat with Expert Mountain Climber:

Pat Clark, Founder of Precision Pro Wash & Sales Boost

About Pat:

Pat Clark got his start in business as the owner of Precision Pro Wash in Duncan, SC. He built that company from nothing, with the help of many people along the way. He started Gutter Butter, providing a product for the exterior cleaning industry, as an opportunity to teach his children the principles of business operation and the importance of giving at a young age. Over the years, Pat has developed a passion for speaking and teaching others. He started Sales Boost in 2018 as an avenue to empower other business owners to reach their goals and live out their "why."

JM: Hey Pat, Thank you so much for joining me around the campfire! I admire everything you have accomplished with Precision Pro Wash and sharing a similar background owning a pressure washing business myself, I have a lot of respect for you. I know you have a lot of experience in gaining new customers, what's your best advice for gaining a ton of new residential customers?

PC: I would say, get out there and whatever marketing you're thinking of doing- 10X it! Because a lot of people's mindset is just to put out 1,000 flyers and keep their fingers crossed that their phone will ring. So for me in the beginning, it was all about boots on the ground. It's cheap and cost-effective marketing. So if you're going to put out 1000 clip flyers or door hangers, put out 10,000! I'll never forget the day I said, "I'm gonna put out 500 flyers", and I threw 500, and I got zero calls. I'm like, Well, it's a good try with 500 people. But when I put 5,000 or 10,000 flyers out, that's when I could really start making sense of things. You can't track 1000 at a high level. You can just barely track 5,000, but you can definitely track 10,000, Then start focusing on your wins and start optimizing your marketing pieces so they convert more.

JM: You bring up a crucial point about the importance of being bold and proactive in marketing efforts. Many people rely on traditional methods like distributing a limited number of flyers and hoping for the best. However, to truly make an impact, it's essential to go beyond that mindset and 10X your marketing efforts. What's your best advice for gaining a ton of new commercial customers?

PC: With commercial businesses, I would say start getting involved in your community because commercial success doesn't happen overnight. For me, commercial work took years to acquire. I had to literally pound the streets and let people know who we were for longer than you would think. It actually took over two years before we landed our first commercial property management company. I was constantly putting in unsolicited proposals, contacting them on holidays, randomly checking in and just doing my best to stay relevant. So for commercial work, I would say get involved in your community and join BOMA, the Building Owners and Managers Association. It costs a decent amount, but it's totally worth it. That investment is going to push you. It will drive you to work harder and to go talk to at least 10 people right away. My business coach told me years ago to find 10 people that'll give you

$100,000 worth of work a year, and you've got a million-dollar business. Then I found one. It took me years of getting my feet wet doing small projects and doing them really, really well. In my first commercial project, I made a point to go above and beyond their expectations. I printed out 250 before and after pictures. I printed all those pictures then went to Walmart on the last day and placed them in a picture book. I gave it to the property manager at the end of the project. I explained our process and showed her exactly how incredibly clean her property turned out. This project was in Mobile, Alabama. The crazy thing is, when I was driving back home on a nine-hour ride to Greenville, SC, an unexpected call came in. The lady calls me and says: We actually gave the picture book to one of our property managers, a regional manager, and they're going to go over it during their next major meeting. The blessing is, we ended up getting a bunch more projects from doing great work from that small act of going above and beyond. The projects were $30,000, $60,000 and $80,000 projects. We were just blown away with that! So what I would say is get impactful in your community and build and nurture commercial relationships like there's no tomorrow!

JM: You hit the nail on the head with this one, Pat. Building a successful commercial clientele requires persistence, relationship-building, and going the extra mile to make a lasting impression. What's the best advice you can give to someone who's looking to retain customers for life?

PC: I like teaching off my experience because we've been in business for 16 years. I have so many stories to tell, but if you want to keep customers for life, you must consider offering a warranty and serving the customers that are your ideal avatar. When I started my business, it started with giving really good prices, but something funny happened. I noticed that when I was doing $200 house washes, those customers weren't coming back, nor did they turn into lifelong customers. They were simply motivated by a cheap price and always went with the next cheapest company. So we started to change things up. We began charging more, and started offering a warranty on our services. We would even give them a warranty certificate at the end of the job. We kept it on file and then we created our mailing list. So we stayed in contact with them four times a year. In the beginning, it's hard, right? Because you're like, how am I supposed to go do estimates, do the work, all while staying in contact? The answer is; the right CRM will help you achieve all of that and more. The great ones make it easy to send out newsletters and mailers with the click of a button. Consider starting by having someone in your office create some monthly items just to stay in front of your customer base. You must 'love up' on your customers. So that could be done with giveaways, gifts, holiday cards and things of that nature. In fact, we send out a postcard with our family on it every year. Believe it or not, your perfect customers follow it, they follow your life, they follow your story. So I always say "sales is a transfer of emotion." When you have loyal customers, it's a transfer of emotion. They've got to buy in on your vision, your company, your goals, your core beliefs, and all that stuff that really matters. So tie it in. I can't tell you how many times they go to my website, and dive into our "About Us" page. And it's the story, right? Coming from literally being a 20-year-old starting this business, not knowing anything about business, then having people believing in you and getting to where we are now really matters. Simply put, the goal is to just stop worrying about the next sale. Instead, be more relationship-driven, then nurture those relationships, 'love up' on them and watch your business skyrocket! Never forget that you own a service company, so serve your people like they are your grandmother.

JM: 16 years in business is no joke! I love the knowledge and expertise you bring to the table. I couldn't agree more that catering to your ideal customers is crucial in cultivating long-term loyalty. By prioritizing customer care and nurturing these relationships, your service company can flourish and experience exponential growth. What are the top 3 most effective ways to gain new customers offline (not on the internet)?

PC: If you're talking about offline, you're talking about right now, in my opinion. Think about it like this- what can you do this week to generate new customers by next week? You know I'm a huge fan of boots on the ground! Almost every business truly starts off with Boots on the Ground efforts. But what happens is, when a service business begins to grow, they typically stop these boots-on-the-ground efforts. Why does this happen? The answer is that we are all human and we humans love to go after the easy stuff. Don't fall into this trap. Stay on working for the community on foot. So my top answer is obviously canvassing flyers because you can get so many out. I'm always looking at quantity because it's a numbers game. I hate to say it that way. But it is a numbers game, then it eventually transitions into a relationship game. So number one is clip flyers for me. Number two is yard signs. You must get a ton of these out constantly. And then number three is Google all day. You must bolt on Google. As a coach, I always ask my students, "Are you hitting on all cylinders?" Clip flyers and yard signs are the one-two punch in my industry. First, they become aware by the flyer then they see the yard sign down the road or in a community. Last, they usually go to Google, look up your reviews and check out your website. I recommend supporting all of this with wrapped vehicles. Never forget that perception is reality and people love to work with larger and well-oiled companies. A cool little trick you can do is label your service vehicles with odd numbers, and your sales vehicles with even numbers. So my trucks are 3,5,7, and 9. I only have four trucks on the road, but it says nine on there like I'm running nine service vehicles. So remember to push your flyers, yard signs, Google efforts and support it all with wrapped vehicles. I know you asked for 3 but I wanted to over deliver!

JM: I appreciate your killer approach to generating new customers and your emphasis on boots-on-the-ground efforts. It's evident that you understand the importance of quantity and numbers as an initial approach, but also recognize the significance of building relationships as your business grows. I'd love to ask, What do service business owners waste too much time on from a marketing perspective?

PC: So I think they get analysis paralysis. People compare themselves to other business owners and try to replicate others, not being mindful that the other businesses might be in a completely different stage of business. Then they want to jump right to stage three, or whatever it is in business. They want to do Google hard. Then they want to use all the shiny gadgets. There's a lot right now you can get lost in. They're like a kid in a candy store with different things. Keep it super simple in the beginning, and then bolt on as you scale. So start small and stay lean and focused. I also see small business owners spend too much time figuring out what flyer to use, or what design should be on a yard sign. Then to top it off, they only put out a few hundred! Remember the power of imperfect action. They get into this owner-operator rut, they market for a week and then stop marketing and go on the truck and work for a whole week! This is the wrong way of thinking. Start your week off right! Market in the morning and the evening. Make sure you're hitting your goal each week and don't go home til your 10X goal is met!

JM: I can relate to that feeling like a kid in a candy store with all different things but the best advice I've ever received was to keep it simple. It's common for business owners to compare themselves to others and try to replicate their strategies without considering the differences in business stages. Such great insight man! Pat, I have one last question before we end this campfire- what type of mindset does it take to grow a successful service business in this day and age?

PC: You must have a mentality that says not doing it is not an option. It must be "go forward" all the time. So it's really all about pure grit. For me, I had $4000 left in my bank account and here's how it went down. I took every dollar from my bank account to pursue the mission, then my mindset was, "I'm all in, and there is no option of failure." Train yourself to know that if you don't think it's going to work, then that means you won't be able to put food on the table for your family, and that's not even close to an option. I remember when I came across the Soft Washing Legend, AC Locklear, and I hired him with the last $4,000 I had in my bank. He then gave me a system to market the right way. It was the rock flyer in the bag. He said, just throw this on the driveway. I'm like, dude, everybody's doing that. And he's like, Yeah, but you need to do it. I was like, alright, so he told me how to do it. Then I literally stayed up countless nights until 11 o'clock pm, chopping the flyers. I made three flyers on a piece of paper. I chopped them, because I couldn't afford to have them chopped. I then put them in bags. I stapled the bag, and I distributed them by myself at 4am every morning. I knew I needed to get a thousand or more per week minimum when I was at that stage. AC eventually said to me: "Dude, it's like Jesus Christ is strapped to your back." Because I was executing. I was following the system. I was putting all I was in that moment. You know what I mean? Like, I had to make it work because it was my last $4,000. Up to that point, I normally made about $5,000 in the month of January. I hired him in December. We ended up doing $15,000 from me just handing out flyers. That's me doing all the work from every angle. Losing was not an option. I had nothing. Now we have 10 locations in 10 different states. God has really blessed us. Always remember, God created birds, but he didn't put food in their nests. They had to go get it!

🔔

Growth Engines designed to add fuel to the fire
(Secondary Lead Sources)

Public Speaking:

Public speaking has traditionally meant the act of speaking face-to-face to a live audience. Today it includes any form of speaking to an audience, including virtual events. Getting in front of your literal audience is extremely powerful and effective. Speak at trade shows, HOA meetings, realtor events and any opportunity where your customer avatar lives. The more people that know you exist, the better. It gives people the perception that you are the local market leader and really offers a major competitive advantage.

Primary mission: Obtain New Business & Networking

How you will make the most money from it: Be very dialed into who your attendees are and tailor your presentation to them. If you are speaking at an HOA Board Meeting, then talk about how your company specializes in HOA properties and why. If you are speaking to a group of realtors, make sure you inform them on how your service will benefit them and will help them get more money for their listings, etc. Call this your Public Speaking System. Test out what works best for your company, document the system and set it in motion.

Host an event:

You have plenty of expertise in your field—why not get involved in the community? By sharing your experience and getting involved in your industry at a local level, you'll have the opportunity to grow your connections, as well as your reputation as a thought leader in your industry.

Primary mission: Obtain New Business & Networking

How you will make the most money from it: You will make the most money by inviting potential customers, vendors, business relationships, and other people you can make money with. Side-note, it's an incredible way to loop in the organizations that you support and mention that all proceeds from ticket sales go to them. Consider hosting a Trunk-or-treat for Halloween, Canned food drive for Thanksgiving and/or collecting presents during the holidays for a Kids with Cancer organization. These are just a few examples but hopefully this gets your wheels turning. Call this your Hosting an Event System. Test out what works best for your company, document the system and set it in motion.

BNI Groups:

BNI stands for Business Networking International. It is the world's leading business referral organization, with nearly 283,000 members in 10,000 chapters worldwide. BNI operates a network of franchises in different territories.

Primary mission: Obtain Referrals & Networking

How you will make the most money from it: Be a networking machine. If you go in with the mindset that your network increases your net worth, then you have a mission to shake as many hands as possible. You never know who you will be meeting and how they can support you and vice versa. Set a monthly target of how many new contacts you make. Add them to your LinkedIn, Facebook and Cell Phone. Plant the seed, water and till it then watch the relationships flourish. Call this your BNI System. Test out what works best for your company, document the system and set it in motion.

Brochure Displays

As the name suggests, a display is meant to hold and display marketing brochures.

Primary mission: Obtain New Business

How you will make the most money from it: As a best practice, keep brochure displays out in your office. Also, make sure to try and leave them at barbershops, restaurants, supply stores or anywhere else your perfect customer avatar might be. Call this your Brochure Display System. Test out what works best for your company, document the system and set it in motion.

Unique to You Tactic:

Every business should strive to be different in a good way. It not only helps to cultivate a place to be creative (hint: nobody wants to work at a boring company), but it separates your organization from the pack. For example, we threw out rock bags and called them bait. They were smaller little baggies, with a folded flyer placed in them and had a catchy saying: "Our price and service rocks!" Similar to clip flyers, the mission was to get out as many as possible on a daily basis. My friend Pat Clark places labels on garden hose spigots that says: "Property Serviced by Precision Pro Wash" and showcases his phone number. It's clever because when Mrs. Jones is trying to find her favorite pressure washing company, she can always just check on the side of her house.

Primary mission: Obtain New Business

How you will make the most money from it: Feel free to run with this idea and spin it if you'd like. If rock bags aren't for you, come up with something that is. Dropping off custom cigars or golf balls with your logo on the wrapper or mousepads to property managers is another example. Call this your Unique To You System. Test out what works best for your company, document the system and set it in motion.

Sweet Treat Prospecting:

One of my favorite creative Relationship Marketing tactics has to do with realtors. Remember, you can go after a one-to-one or one-to-many approach when acquiring new customers. When we went to build out our realtor system, we realized that if we did this right, realtors would be recommending us like crazy. Remember, they also benefit when the property is spotless and as clean as possible. Ask any realtor, and they will tell you, a clean and pristine property outsells a dirty one every day of the week. So what we had were delicious, custom cookies with our logo designed on there and distributed them on a quarterly basis. We would also print out and sign a stack of letters that introduced our company and why we were experts at working with realtors. We would talk with their lingo and mention we were aware that if properties were spotless, it would be an easier sell for them, and they would drastically increase their close rate by partnering with a company like ours. The last thing we left were business cards or magnet business cards that they could hold onto when the cookies were gone. Every quarter we would drop off two dozen cookies to every local real estate office in a 45-mile radius of our headquarters. We would call all of the realtor offices ahead of time and let them know we would be stopping in and would love to drop off a gift for all the realtors in the office that day. Then we would show up, do our best to do an impromptu presentation about who we were and why they should use us, shake some hands and always hear the famous line: "This is brilliant! I never thought of printing a logo on a cookie and writing a personalized letter to someone I want to do business with." It worked like a charm, and nobody did more business with realtors than us.

Primary mission: Obtain New Business and Referrals

How you will make the most money from it: Create a contact list of every real estate office in your service area. Get custom cookies made with your logo on top. Create a flyer that talks about how your company is the "go to" experts in partnering with realtors and explain why. Drop off a dozen cookies or so, a stack of the custom flyers and business cards to every real estate office 2-4 times a year. Try to force a quick presentation for any realtors that might be in the office, just introducing yourself, your company and the reason for stopping by. If you can't get a quick presentation, grab the realtor's business card and send them a follow-up email saying you hope they enjoy the cookies and that you are looking forward to building a relationship with them. Call this your Sweet Treat System. Test out what works best for your company, document the system and set it in motion.

Memberships / Trade Associations:

Trade associations play an important role in the home service industry. A trade association is a voluntary organization of independent business units in the same branch of industry, which conducts co-operative activities aimed at improving the welfare of the group. The strong and credible ones protect and promote the interests of their members on many levels. Their mission includes educating members to strengthen the industry and offering support in several areas.

Primary mission: Obtain New Business, Boost Credibility & Education

How you will make the most money from it: If you join the right ones, you will learn more, build a better network and boost your credibility. Spend time analyzing the trade associations in your field and spend time weighing out the pros and cons of each. Join one and see how you like it. You're not married to it so just go in with an open mind and see how it can help you grow. Just make sure the one you join will help you add value and revenue to your business. For example, some associations will teach you tactful ways to land more commercial work and service them on a contract basis. Your small membership fee will really pay off in this case. Many play politics so just be a student of the game prior to aligning your company with any negative organizations. Call this your Membership / Trade Association System. Test out what works best for your company, document the system and set it in motion.

Refrigerator Magnets:

Personalized business card magnets make highly effective marketing tools as these are well-retained and will keep your message and name displayed in front of your customers for a very long time. There is no better feeling than when a long-time customer contacts you and says: "I've kept your magnet on my fridge forever. Can you come take care of my home?" If you have experience with handing out magnets, then you know how often this happens. Talk about a massive ROI and an incredible way to lower customer acquisition costs. It's clever because this is an old school method that many overlook. They are pretty inexpensive so this is a must in my book.

Primary mission: Obtain Repeat Business

How you will make the most money from it: Give one to every customer you serve. Tell them to place it on their fridge and that you look forward to being their go-to company for life. Call this your Magnet System. Test out what works best for your company, document the system and set it in motion.

Local Publications:

Local publications are localized print mediums distributed in select areas. Certain publications still play an important role in today's market. The right publications are super effective if the readership is solid. For example, if there is a local home service magazine that's mailed to 50k homes in prestigious neighborhoods and you have an effective ad in there, it might be worth it to you. Don't discount this strategy until you give it an effective test. Some publications don't yield much of an ROI while others will drive in a ton of calls.

Primary mission: Obtain New Business & Branding

How you will make the most money from it: Purchase Ad Space in a magazine that your customer avatar reads or thumbs through on a regular basis. I suggest one of the magazines that get mailed to the homes you service already, if possible, since your brand is relevant in this area. Do a minimum of a 6 month run (during your busy season. Never test a new lead source during the down months) and then run a Monthly Marketing Report against it. Try to position your ad in a prime spot (Cover, Front Inside Cover, Back Inside Cover and Back get the most eyeballs on it). Don't be afraid to call the publisher and ask if you can be a contributor to the publication. If you publish a monthly article on how to keep your pool clean, clear your A/C drain line, maintain your yard or other topics relevant to your niche, people will begin to trust you which if done right, will lead to more business. Call this your Local Publication System. Test out what works best for your company, document the system and set it in motion.

Direct Mail:

A type of direct marketing that's delivered physically to a prospect's mailbox through the United States Postal Service or other delivery service.

Primary mission: Obtain New Business, Branding & Repeat Business

How you will make the most money from it: Do not send direct mail randomly. They should be sent strategically throughout the year when business is predictably slow. An example would be sending out a large postcard a few weeks prior to the start of your season, offering a limited-time special if they book by a certain date. The goal of direct mail should be to fill capacity and ensure it's always running at 100%. I don't advise that you make direct mail or print mediums your only way of sourcing leads but build it into your overall marketing game-plan for sure. Call this your Direct Mail System. Test out what works best for your company, document the system and set it in motion.

Maintenance Contracts:

Maintenance contracts are agreements made between your company and the customer to service the property on a scheduled basis. Recurring contracts can be game-changing for your bottom line. They create more predictable income, offer more reassurance to employees and support scale. There's nothing quite like promised money in the home service business. Every single service company should figure out how to implement one or multiple recurring services into their business model.

Primary mission: Obtain Repeat Business

How you will make the most money from it: Offer a one-time initial service price, and then a discounted rate to come back and maintain it multiple times per year. Additionally, if you ever want to sell your business, residual income is a major benefit for a potential buyer as it drastically mitigates investment risks. You can also automate this process by having an email sequence go out to the customer's post transaction, explaining the whole offer. This will sell itself if you knock the initial service out of the park. Call this your Maintenance Contract System. Test out what works best for your company, document the system and set it in motion.

Billboards:

A billboard is a large outdoor advertising structure, typically found in high-traffic areas such as busy roads and highways. Billboards present large advertisements to passing pedestrians and drivers. Typically, companies use billboards to build their brands or to get leads to pour in.

Primary mission: Obtain New Business

How you will make the most money from it: Ensure that the billboard you want has the eyeballs of your perfect customer on there. If you do a billboard simply as an ego-flex, you won't get a great ROI. If you do it in an area where your perfect customer sees it often, the branding is on point and the offer and call to action are dialed in, it has a higher chance of success. Call this your Billboard System. Test out what works best for your company, document the system and set it in motion.

Digital Vehicle Billboards:

A mobile billboard, also known as a "digital billboard truck" is a device used for advertising on the sides of a truck or trailer that is typically mobile. Using a mobile billboard for advertising is an advertising niche called Mobile Outdoor Advertising. It's effective because it's dynamic, and you could change out the text as much as you'd like to tailor your message to each season or offer.

Primary mission: Obtain New Business

How you will make the most money from it: I don't recommend advertising on mobile ad trucks. I do, however, believe that having digital signage on one or more of your vehicles is a way to really stand out and be remembered. It's completely out of the box and that's why I like it. Call this your Digital Vehicle Billboard System. Test out what works best for your company, document the system and set it in motion.

Bus Stop Advertising:

Bus stop advertising can achieve targeted awareness and is easily combined with other advertising formats, such as billboards and buses, giving maximum exposure to your services. A large percentage of bus stops are 6ft by 4ft and are illuminated 24/7. They don't get the phone to ring like crazy but all it takes is one heavy hitter to see it and the juice is worth the squeeze.

Primary mission: Obtain New Business & Branding

How you will make the most money from it: If you find the right bus stop or bench that your perfect customer sees daily, it has the ability to yield an ROI. In my experience, the best returns typically come from stops located near a school where people need to drive slowly. Call this your Bus Stop System. Test out what works best for your company, document the system and set it in motion.

QR Codes:

QR codes can provide more information about your services with the click of a button. Basically, QR codes promote interaction and engagement through mobile phones. This type of marketing strategy enables businesses to transfer information to the user by scanning a unique code which can point the user to a specific page on your website or somewhere else. If done right, it will boost your inbound form submissions such as leads or job applications.

Primary mission: Obtain New Business & Website Form Submissions

How you will make the most money from it: Get a QR code on your marketing collateral that drives visitors to a specific web page. If you are passing out flyers to a realtor, have a QR embedded on there, so that when realtors scan it, it drives them to your "Why Realtors Choose Us" page. It is also a clever way to get more applications if you have the code in places where your ideal employees might be. You can also have QR codes on vehicles, apparel, yard signs or anywhere else mobile phones can capture them. I used the realtor as a good example but this initiative can be rolled out in countless ways. Call this your QR Code System. Test out what works best for your company, document the system and set it in motion.

Sponsorships:

Most people like to support local, independent businesses. Raise your status in your community by participating in charity events and organizations. Sponsorships are an incredible way to financially support the organizations you chose on your Community Impact List.

Primary mission: Obtain New Business, Branding, Supports Giving Initiative

How you will make the most money from it: Sponsor a local fun run, organize a holiday "toys for kids" drive, or supply a Little League team in your city with equipment. All this raises your profile, which helps attract new customers. Charities always hold events and could use your support. Start thinking of what organizations you'd like to align your business with moving forward and execute on sponsoring. Call this your Sponsorship System. Test out what works best for your company, document the system and set it in motion.

Public Relations:

Public relations, aka PR, is often overlooked in small businesses. Securing local and/or major media coverage is a really big deal for any small business. It increases your brand awareness and visibility, which always leads to more revenue and more trust. More eyeballs on your business equate to more statistical traffic on your website. It also improves your reputation and gives your friends, family and employees a moment to share the flex. Here's an example: "Hey look, it's Jon on TV. It looks like he and his company are painting a ton of buildings for Habitat for Humanity here in South Florida." I only say this for one reason. People love supporting their friends when things pop up on social media from my experience. In turn, will boost the sharing component. For me, a simple act of serving and helping an organization in need is more than enough. However, I must always remind myself that I am operating a business to ring the bell, so this moment has the ability to create more revenue, but more importantly, it really speaks to deepening your impact on this world.

Primary mission: Obtain New Business & Branding, Supports Giving Initiative

How you will make the most money from it: Take the video clip from the local news station and spread it like wildfire all over social media. Also, get the clip up on your website to increase credibility and trust with your website visitors. The most important thing you can do is build relationships with connections at news stations, magazines and other relevant outlets and get on their radar several times throughout the year, every year. Call this your PR System. Test out what works best for your company, document the system and set it in motion.

Corporate Letters of Recommendation:

Letters of Recommendation matter from large corporate companies if you are on the hunt for repetitive, residual agreements. For example, if someone in a leadership position from a local grocery store such as Publix takes the time to type up a personalized letter about how incredible your company is, you would be able to use that as a marketing piece to obtain more grocery store business. It's all about getting these powerful assets in your arsenal that will ultimately help you gain more business.

Primary mission: Obtain New Business & Boost Credibility

How you will make the most money from it: Either yourself or your sales team should get in front of every important corporate chain in your region, force a sales presentation and showcase your Letters of Recommendation along with the pictures and videos you shot during your previous corporate service project. Then it's all about leverage. Once you've got other like minded businesses vouching for you- you can go get more business in that niche. This is one of my favorite outside of the box strategies on dominating the market on the commercial side. Call this your Letters of Recommendation System. Test out what works best for your company, document the system and set it in motion.

24/7 Answering Service:

In the simplest sense, 24/7 support means providing your customers with live help at all times. Having a live person answer your phone 24 hours a day, 7 days a week, can be super beneficial for your business. This person or company can read your greeting script and answer basic questions, so your company doesn't miss a single phone call. If they are next level, they are able to offer estimates and troubleshoot basic customer concerns that inevitably pop up from time to time.

Primary mission: Obtain New Business & Enhance Customer Experience

How you will make the most money from it: Potential customers hate it when service companies do not answer their phones. You can make the most money from this by having the operator collect any potential lead info after hours and have them email it to you. If the lead is worth your time, you can contact them immediately before they continue the hunt to hire your competition. Call this your Answering Service System. Test out what works best for your company, document the system and set it in motion.

Radio Ads:

Radio advertising is any advertising effort featured via AM, FM, satellite, or online radio. Radio advertising remains a cost-effective solution for reaching large audiences, exposing them to your brand and your services.

Primary mission: Obtain New Business & Branding

How you will make the most money from it: First, make sure the ads target your perfect customer. Next, make sure the ad has a captivating opening hook, is unique and offers a powerful call to action. If you plan on running radio ads as part of your marketing calendar moving forward, consider integrating a jingle into the advertisement, as the jingle historically helps to increase conversion rates. Call this your Radio Ads System. Test out what works best for your company, document the system and set it in motion.

Television Commercials:

Television advertising is similar to radio advertising in the sense of relaying a specific sales pitch in a limited amount of time. Most television ads are either 30 or 60 seconds in duration, long enough to give the viewers pertinent information or create a specific opinion of the product or service, but not long enough to lose the viewer's attention. Historically, tv commercials are pretty costly so the only way I would do it is if you got an incredible deal and/or if your service industry offers high tickets such as HVAC, Roofing and Plumbing. Television commercials are generally placed at strategic breaks during the main programming and the few minutes until the top of the next hour.

Primary mission: Obtain New Business & Branding

How you will make the most money from it: The commercial needs to be unique, catchy and always have a strong call to action. Call this your TV Commercial System. Test out what works best for your company, document the system and set it in motion.

Neighborhood TV Channel:

This is a dedicated channel for people who live in a specific community or subdivision. It's largely popular in senior communities where people don't use the internet as much but still want to learn about the "happenings" going on in their neighborhoods and the surrounding areas. This isn't a major money maker but it is important that your business is always in front of your perfect customer.

Primary mission: Obtain New Business & Branding

How you will make the most money from it: Find out which communities have tv channels and see what it would take to get a listing on there if that's where your customer avatar resides. Call this your Neighborhood TV System. Test out what works best for your company, document the system and set it in motion.

ONLINE GROWTH ENGINE SOFTWARE

Online Software designed to support and advance growth engines

Artificial Intelligence Software:

Artificial Intelligence (AI) Software is a computer program which mimics human behavior by learning various data patterns and insights. Top features of AI software include Machine Learning, Speech & Voice Recognition, Virtual Assistant tasks and more. AI has emerged as a game-changing technology: systems that can perform complex tasks typically requiring human intelligence, such as speech recognition, decision-making, and content creation. With its capability to automate processes and personalize experiences, AI, including platforms such as ChatGPT, has become an invaluable asset for businesses of all sizes.

Primary mission: Education, Marketing and Time Saver. It's ability to understand natural language and have a text conversation with people ensures it will collapse time.

How you will make the most money from it: For small businesses, AI offers three strategic advantages to enhance customer service, strengthen marketing and sales, and drive growth. These are Customer Experience, Marketing and Content. From creating graphics to websites, marketing campaigns to blog content- the right AI will drastically fast forward many tasks for you. Start using this software to pump out informational content that you can showcase to your customers (Checklists, DIY Tips, etc.) Once you get the hang of it, go deeper and leverage it further in every way possible.

Review Generation Software:

Easily and effectively get more authentic customer reviews. Use the voice of the customer to show you provide the best experience in your local market. Get more reviews from your customers via email, SMS, on your website and on your social channels.

Primary mission: Obtain New Online Reviews

How you will make the most money from it: Build out your Review Generation System. For example, after each job, ensure your office or technician sends your satisfied customer a request for a review. If they fill it out, it's mission complete. If they don't, the review software will work in a text and/or email sequence to obtain the review conversion.

SMS Text Message Software:

Text message marketing uses SMS (Short Message Service) or text messages to deliver promotional messages to customers and subscribers. Businesses use text message marketing to increase brand awareness, generate sales, provide news to subscribers, increase web traffic or run promotions. Unlike email marketing, Mrs. Jones has no choice but to see your message. As you're reading this book, you might have received an email that fell into your inbox. Something's telling me it did not derail you from your mission of reading or listening to this. Now say you're reading this book or listening to it on audio as we speak, and your phone vibrates, and the notification goes off. What are you going to do? Exactly my point! You are going to be forced to look at that message whether you like it or not. This type of push marketing is extremely effective, and it converts like crazy.

Primary mission: Obtain Repeat Business

How you will make the most money from it: I highly suggest using any of the software listed above and applying my highest converting text template when you are ready to go. My best advice is to not deploy text software unless you have the capacity to fill and you can execute and fulfill all of the new requests that come in. Learn from me, never deploy your text to your entire database or even half of your database at once. Do it measurably. Do it in segmented rounds of 100 or 200 until you understand what type of return you'll get. If you can, segment the list by zip code so you don't need to travel too far. The last thing you want to do is send a text out of good faith to 20,000 past customers offering them a discount for their loyalty. And then the 5000 of those customers write back over the next few days and you can't fulfill the request.

Pro Tip: Here's my highest-performing template:

"Good morning, it's Jon from ABC Service Company- I hope all is well! Wanted to let you know I'll be in your neck of the woods next week. I can give you 20% off any services since I won't have any travel costs. Can I get you on the schedule?"

It's simple, effective and here's why. It immediately tells Mrs. Jones that she knows me and this implies trust and disarms her. It checks in on her well-being and people appreciate you caring about them. It tells her that serving her will be an easy and efficient process. It gets her on your side by beating her to the punch by offering a great discount. It drives quick action by pressing an urgent, limited-time offer with only being in her neighborhood next week. It ends by implying that because we have a great relationship and I'll take good care of her. When it comes to turning on beast mode and killing SMS Text Blasts, less is more. Just make sure your message is crafted to disarm, gets the customer on your side, has a compelling offer and assumes the sale.

Email Marketing Software:

Email marketing is the act of sending a message, typically to a group of people, using email. It involves using email to send advertisements, request business or solicit sales. The power of email marketing is something that should not be overlooked in your quest to dominate the market. There are several reasons why I enjoy email marketing but my first reason is because it's a really good tool for building strong customer relationships. Your customers appreciate knowing that you were thinking about them. Believe it or not, many of them want to be made aware of the latest happenings in your business. It's your job to keep them up-to-date. The second reason I love email marketing is because it's super cost-effective. For companies that are in major growth mode, it's a huge way to drive new business and drive forward your brand for very little spend. I also really enjoy the fact that email marketing is a way to give your company a unique voice. It gives you a direct line to inboxes, and you can craft your style and imagery to the best of your ability. I say it quite often, but there is so much power in automation. You can set up automatic campaigns to deploy at certain times as well as set up nurture sequences so your emails can navigate a sale or action in a very specific manner. Last but not least, it creates a lot of credibility in your business when you are staying in front of your customers methodically. I do believe that email marketing is a really solid tool to acquire new business, but I love how the consistency of emails and email newsletters drives home credibility and trust within a brand. After all, what do people do when they believe you are the real deal and trust you over the next guy? That's right, they buy from you. Dollar for dollar, email marketing is one of the most affordable ways to market your business. In my opinion, every home service business should be doing at least one email per month.

Primary mission: Obtain New & Repeat Business

How you will make the most money from it: Create an email creative and upload your database. Then send the email to them! If this is your first time email marketing, make it a friendly greeting saying hello to your customers and attach a compelling offer. If you have advanced to automation and sequences, just carefully think through everything before you deploy it. There's a fine line between staying on top of your customers mind and being way too much that it earns you a quick unsubscribe.

Ringless Voicemail Software:

Ringless voicemail, also called a voicemail drop, is a method in which a pre-recorded audio message is placed in a voicemail inbox without the associated telephone ringing first. Have you ever walked away from your mobile phone or returned a few minutes later to see that you have a voicemail on your screen? Or how about when your phone is right next to you, and you see a voicemail pop up? Human behavior tells us immediately that we missed the call. How did this happen? The answer is Ringless voicemails! Ringless voicemails are powerful and yield a fantastic ROI. The way it works is much easier than you would imagine. You simply log into a software platform and initiate the platform to give you a call. Once an automatic dialer reaches you, you simply record a greeting. Next, the recording essentially gets saved into the voicemail platform and then you can deploy it. Be very mindful because just like SMS text messaging, if you do this right, you will not be able to handle all of the return phone calls and fulfill all of your orders.

Primary mission: Obtain Repeat Business

How you will make the most money from it: Send a Ringless Voicemail when you need to fill gaps in your schedule or fill capacity.

My highest performing template: "Hey! It's Jon from ABC Service Company. Hope all is well! Wanted to let you know that I will be in your neighborhood all of next week and would be happy to help get anything cleaned that you might need while I'm in there. You know I'll certainly take care of you since I don't need to add any travel costs. Give me a quick call back to let me know if I should get you on the schedule. Talk soon!"

CRM Software:

Customer relationship management is a process in which a business administers its interactions with customers. A CRM system essentially provides a central place where businesses can store customer and prospect data, track customer interactions, and helps automate and level up the customer experience on many levels.

Primary mission: Manage Leads & Nurture Database

How you will make the most money from it: Most of these platforms offer a free trial so jump in and test out which is the best fit for your business. Utilize these platforms and explore the features and integrations thoroughly. Keep in mind, a business is only as strong as its data, so make sure you have incredible customer information and notes kept. Think about how grateful the future you will be if you ever decide to sell your business.

Automatic Bidding Software:

Automatic bidding software is gaining in popularity every single year. Essentially, rather than a simple contact form on your website, an automated bidding form will estimate and close the deal for you. In a nutshell, automatic bidding software productizes your service offerings, and the intelligent software actually sells and closes for you through automation. Historically speaking, you should see an increase in customer satisfaction, higher ticket prices and a boost in close rates.

Primary mission: Obtain New Business

How you will make the most money from it: Test it out to see if it fits into your business model. Some companies prefer selling deals themselves, and others opt to have their bidding forms do it for them. You can actually blend your model and still have traditional salespeople do in-person estimates leveraging the software as well.

Live Chat Software:

Live chat is a form of customer messaging software that allows customers to speak directly with a company representative. It's a very effective messaging system for small businesses which works as a pop-up chat window within a company's website. I love it because it enhances the website visitors experience as well as functions as a way to pick off real-time traffic on your website.

Primary mission: Obtain New Business & Enhance Customer Service

How you will make the most money from it: Use a live chat plugin or a real company that offers the service on your website. The right tool will open up conversions and lead flow even further.

Call Tracking Software:

Call tracking software tracks and records information from incoming phone calls, including call source and audio recordings. It enables businesses and marketers to attribute phone calls to the marketing channels that drove them, such as pay-per-call, local SEO, and other online and offline call-based marketing campaigns.

Primary mission: Attribute Leads & Enhance Customer Service

How you will make the most money from it: This is the most powerful way to track your inbound phone call leads to help you better gauge ROI. Enable whisper messages to inform you where each lead originates from. An example of a whisper message, when the phone rings, you hear: "Call from Google Ads."

TRACK & MEASURE SUCCESS

The growth engines I just mentioned will help you make more money than ever. But this book isn't about just spending in every area possible and waiting for leads to flood in. It's about being the best marketer and business owner possible. That's why you need to stay laser-focused on your ROI. I touched on the fact that it should be 5 to 1 or better in order to keep it going. Let me elaborate on this for a minute to offer some clarity. Some marketing activities don't just yield an instant 5 to 1 return. In fact, it's the complete opposite in the case of Google Ads. Agencies like mine put powerful measures in place to make sure you are converting at a high level as soon as possible. However, once the floodgates open, it's inevitable that month-over-month optimizations need to occur. Google Ads is constantly changing, and so is your customers' search behavior online. That's why campaigns need to be optimized on a regular basis. Just know that after 90 days, if you aren't somewhere in the stratosphere of a healthy ROI, there is either an issue in the Ads account, issue in the local market and/or an issue in your sales teams closing ability. Be mindful of seasonality, inclement weather, presidential campaigns, back-to-school distractions and other events that are taking place during your campaign, as they predictably slow down the lead flow.

Also, remember that some marketing activities, such as television commercials or trade shows, traditionally don't pull in an immediate return on investment. These mediums historically add a ton of value on the back-end or in the long game. These customers are valuable as well because once you close and serve them, you have the ability to retain them for life. They become known as a Customer Lifetime Value play. CLV is a business metric that measures how much a business can plan to earn from the average customer over the course of the relationship.

When it comes to tracking and measuring your efforts, you only need a handful of tools to gauge success. The first item you will need to have in place, is call and form tracking. A company such as Call Rail or Call Tracking Metrics offers robust tracking across the board. The second item you will need in place is ensuring your administrative team is trained and ready to field and schedule inbound calls. As soon as the inbound call comes in, your staff should greet the potential customer in a friendly manner, asking where they found you and proceeding with the estimate. If you only have an answering service handling your calls, that's fine too, but they should be capturing those important data points for you. You can't measure what you don't track, so do not let this slip through the cracks. The third item you will need is excellent reporting. If you have a solid marketing agency running the show behind the scenes, then there's a great chance that they have great reporting and/or a real-time dashboard for you to log into and see your real-time results. The fourth item you will need is called a "Monthly Marketing Report" and this is easy to create. Create a simple document that lists out all of the Growth Engines you are using on a monthly basis in one column. Then next to it, list how much revenue *was generated* per engine that month and divide it by how much *was spent* on the engine that month. That's it! It will show you your ROI in real time.

Here's an example:

Growth Engine = Google Ads

Monthly Revenue Generated = $50,000

Monthly Spend = $5,000

TOTAL ROI: 10X

Applying these simple tracking methods will help you have a visual of your dollar-for-dollar ROI. Make sure you are analyzing your data the first week of the following month. This way, you can get the most accurate ROI gauge possible from the previous month.

CELEBRATE YOUR WINS

Lewis Howes says: "Treat every small victory like you just won the Super Bowl." Do yourself a huge favor and keep track of all the small wins and losses you incur. The small wins deserve to be acknowledged and celebrated. Are you gaining a 9 to 1 ROI on Google Ads? Buy your company lunch and share the great news. Are you getting a huge return on passing out clip flyers? Let your canvassing team know how much you appreciate them by giving them a $50 gift card to their favorite restaurant. Proud of yourself for making things happen on the marketing side? Get yourself the pair of shoes or the sunglasses that you've wanted so badly.

"Treat every small victory like you just won the Super Bowl."

Lewis Howes

Celebrate your wins, no matter how big or small they might be. On the flip side, if you are hitting some brick walls or generating some failures, acknowledge them and figure out why. Don't play the victim and walk around with a "poor me" attitude. Turn off your emotions, call yourself out and get back to the grind until things start to connect. Always remember, failure is part of the equation that leads to major success. I've failed more times than I can count. When it happens, pick yourself up, dust yourself off and be determined to turn your adversity into your advantage.

TAKE ACTION:

1. Visit JonMajak.com/RingTheBell to download and fill out the "Ring the Bell for Money- Growth Engine Document System"

2. Keep all of these documents handy. As we progress through the book, I'll teach you how to add them to your marketing calendar, where we can then execute on them.

CHAPTER 7:
HOW YOU RING IT FOR IMPACT

*A*s you continuously ring the bell at the top of the mountain, you notice business owners and employees coming out of their offices and staring. Children at school seem to be frozen in awe. Pastors, Rabbis, and religious leaders stepped out of their places of worship and couldn't help but wonder what was going on. Then your body gives out and you fall to the dirt. That's when you lay there in complete exhaustion and your mind recalibrates.

You start thinking of what matters most- your family, loved ones, making a difference, and for the first time in a while, yourself. You notice you're completely covered in blood and sweat. In fact, your hands are completely raw. This last moment of ringing the bell is the most painful, but the most important. After working so hard to stand out for others, you are seeing the world with so much clarity, and your purpose elevates to the next level.

I absolutely love this part of the business with every ounce of my being. For me, business is much more than just making money. Martin Luther King, Jr. famously said, "Life's most persistent and urgent question is: "What are you doing for others?" It's so true because too many people think about themselves far too often when the secret to real happiness happens when you make others feel good. In my humble opinion, what I believe he meant by this quote is that the meaning of life is service. I must preface this chapter by saying there is one important word to hold close to you as you read on. That word is dedication. You must work towards building and turning serving strategies into habits, and this is where mindset comes in hard. What you really need to do is turn your "shoulds" into "musts." You no longer "should" be building your culture, but you "must" in order to create the best company possible. You no longer "should" be touching base with the people that you love the most but you "must" touch base with them to ensure you stay dedicated to showing up in their lives. There are so many ways that you could do this. People say that you can't help everyone in life, but I believe that you can do your best to show up for as many people as possible, including yourself, before your time is up. Outside of how you impact your customers, here's a list of the people that you will undoubtedly impact when you ring the bell.

"Life's most persistent and urgent question is; What are you doing for others?"

Martin Luther King, Jr.

Your Team:

This includes yourself, employees and professional relationships. These should include the people who love and support you the most. Be careful in this process, and make sure you not only select the correct people but you're dedicated to showing up in these people's lives consistently.

Yourself:

The funny thing about being an entrepreneur and a mission-driven leader is the best ones never put themselves first. In fact, it's usually the complete opposite. We, as high-performing leaders, must always put ourselves last. And that's what leads me to a really special part of ringing the bell. This part is all about you, the entrepreneur. As many of you know, this journey is one of the toughest in the entire world. It's full of doubt, fear, dread, walking into the unknown, embarrassment, shame, guilt, anxiety, depression, and countless other painful emotions. But when you are intentional about ringing the bell, things start to change for you. And I'm not talking about temporary change. I'm talking about lasting change that you quite literally earned. When I started my business, I had nothing. Literally nothing. I could barely afford to eat and pay my bills, and was a walking embarrassment in my own mind. At least, that's how I felt. I feel like the world doubted me, and they had every right to. Then one day, everything made sense.

All of those seeds I planted for years on end, started sprouting. All of those hands I shook and phone calls I made, ended up building real relationships. All of those investments I made into my company started paying off. When you ring the bell for yourself, you won't hear or feel the impact for quite some time. But when that impact finally reaches you, it hits hard. It hits so hard that you realize everything you always prayed for is actually the life you are living. Money is no longer an issue, whatever toys or material things you want, you can get. Your savings and investments finally start to grow after years of looking as dry as a desert. You can take a vacation wherever you want, stay in whatever hotel you want, eat at any restaurant you want and buy whatever you want. It really does happen just like that.

One of the greatest blessings I've ever encountered was when my wife got sick, and I had to stay home for close to a year. I had to shift my entire life to taking care of my wife, pulling my son out of school because he couldn't catch any illnesses and bring it home to her fragile immune system. It would have done serious damage to her. Somehow, my business was impacting me so much that I was able to work from home and care for my family while my automated business continued to grow. Never in a million years could I have ever wished for something like that to actually come to fruition. But it did. It was able to pay for hospital visits, ambulance rides, supplements, doctor's visits and countless other things. I was able to support a wife who was unable to work, pay our mortgage, put food on the table, and provide the most important thing of all, hope. Without my business impacting our lives the way it did, we would have been hopeless. Instead, we were able to focus on getting her well, and it transformed me along the way. I got stronger in mind and in body. When you ring the bell with intention, you finally get to do what you probably never did in the past, and that is to show up for yourself. This is priceless.

How to make the greatest impact on yourself: It all begins and ends with having a crystal clear picture of what success looks like. Write out your life and business goals for the next 1 year, 3 years, 5 years and 10 years. Then print out pictures that coincide with the goals and pin them to a large vision board.

System needed: Accountability partner, coach or mentor that knows your goals and has no problem holding you accountable. If you thrive off positive reinforcement, then celebrate your small wins with something that makes you happy such as a massage or buy yourself something you've been wanting. If you are motivated by consequence (like me), then you need hard accountability. For example, if you don't hit your short-term targets, you must write an embarrassing poem about your inability to execute and post it on social media. Another consequence that got me moving was eating one of the spiciest chips known to man, called the 1-chip challenge. You better believe I'm hitting my accountabilities when consequences are my motivator.

Employees:

I can't stress the importance of pouring into your team and company culture. I actually hate the word employee and very much prefer the word co-worker. But for all intents and purposes, I'll use the word employee so it makes practical sense throughout this section. Believe it or not, your team really looks up to you. They may not tell you in that exact way but trust me, they do. Owning an excellent business comes with great responsibility. You are in the driver's seat of so many people's lives. From helping others pay their bills, covering their health insurance needs, helping to put food on the table, helping to put gas in their car, helping to create a plan for them to eventually retire one day, to helping them to take care of their family and travel this beautiful world, it's up to you to make it happen. Sounds a bit scary, right? The truth of the matter is the weight is heavy. But if you made it this far in the book, something tells me that you were built to carry the load. Great work for leveling up your mindset and taking your life and business seriously! Your team literally depends on you to make it happen. When things get extra challenging, just remind yourself to be still, take a deep breath and remember that you were built for this. My father always told me, "It's not easy being the king of the castle. In fact, it's quite the opposite son. But God only entrusts his strongest children with this responsibility, so toughen up and own it."

So that's why a key component of ringing the bell is to make sure you are creating a lasting impact for your employees. They need a safe place where they can grow, and also, when life throws hardships at them, they need a place that supports them. The world is cruel enough, and a leader makes sure their business is a place where employees feel trusted, valued, and safe. Without your team, you have no business. I'm sure they're many business owners reading this right now that might be thinking: "I will never depend on my team, and I will never go to that next level of making them feel loved and appreciated." Unfortunately for you, the sand in the hourglass is coming to an end, and it's only a matter of time until each one of your team members fade away into the abyss. But if you love, care and respect your team at the highest level, they will be as loyal to you as your best friend in the entire world. We didn't win the top spot in Inc. Magazine Best Workplaces in the entire country because we put out the perception that we cared. We actually cared and always will.

How to make the greatest impact on your employees: Put energy into asking them how they're doing. Check in on their mental health, and encourage them to make sure they are taking care of their minds and bodies. Make sure you are helping them earn more as the business measurably grows. Make an effort to organize fun culture-based events such as 5k runs, restaurant outings, company lunches and celebrating work anniversaries. Make sure you are genuine in your effort and not doing things with selfishness at the forefront. When you offer health insurance, dig into it and make sure you get the right plans, and your team can really benefit from the packages you choose. Don't just check a box and tell yourself you've got health insurance. When you say you value your team and their time, don't just say it. Celebrate their birthdays, work anniversaries, the huge moments in their life and show up for the painful moments as well. Death or loss of a loved one isn't easy for anyone. Be the person your team can truly count on. You must walk it like you talk it.

System needed: You are the CEO of your business which means you need to spend time leading the company to the promised land. That means that the system you need is a dedicated employee to run point on this. Whether it's your assistant, a marketing specialist, a business partner or an HR Director, someone needs to be in front of you to ensure you don't miss a beat. Whether you like it or not, everything lives and dies at the feet of the CEO, so make sure your culture is thriving, and your team members are living their best lives.

Professional Relationships:

These relationships include my circle of influence, professional colleagues, people in your leadership groups, fellow coaches, mentors and mentees and suppliers/vendors. I won't be mad at you if you slip a friendly competitor or two into this mix too. Healthy competition is a really good thing.

Everyone should have a circle of influence in their life. These are the people who drive you to level up and would hold you accountable with tough love because they want to see you be the best version of yourself. For me, it's my business partner, my fellow coaches, people in my mastermind groups and others that root for me unconditionally.

Your suppliers and vendors work hard for you and help provide a high-quality product to your customers. They are often overlooked, but if you take a step back and think intentionally for a second, you wouldn't be able to thrive without them. Therefore, you must make an impact in their lives.

Why bring competitors along for the ride on your team? It's simple, because the best ones drive you further, and it also gives you another moment to serve someone else. Right now, there is some local company in your market that really looks up to you whether you believe it or not. Whether they like your branding, your trucks, your approach to business, your operational methods, the way you market, or several other factors, there is someone that could grow from your wisdom. I believe one of the greatest tests you were given as a business owner is whether you kept the cards close to your chest or actually turned them over, smiled and said, "Let's win together." I've made millions of dollars by turning my cards towards the competition and extending a helping hand. There is plenty of business for everyone.

How to make the greatest impact on your professional relationships: My best advice is to wholeheartedly support your professional team. Be a light in their lives and check and see what you can do to help them be the best versions of themselves. Never do anything if you are expecting a favor in return. Be mindful of what matters to them, such as their birthdays, special occasions, holidays and be relentless and show up for them. Thank them often and bonus them accordingly. I've never met an employee, professional relationship, or supplier who was ungrateful for receiving a handwritten thank you card with a gift card included for a nice dinner.

System needed: You need someone in your corner who helps advance this. Consider hiring an assistant or delegating some activities to a dedicated member of your staff that will push you to be a relationship building monster. A digital calendar such as Google Calendar works perfectly here. When (not if) you do this right, you or someone on your team will be in your calendar daily to make sure professional relationships are growing.

Campfire Chat with Expert Mountain Climber:

Debbie Sardone, Founder of Buckets & Bows Maid Service & Cleaning For A Reason (Nonprofit)

About Debbie: Debbie Sardone is a popular consultant, trainer, speaker, author and business owner. Described as a "serial entrepreneur" she owns several successful businesses, including Buckets & Bows Maid Service, her residential cleaning business, and Speed Cleaning, a manufacturer and distributor of premium green cleaning products and professional- grade cleaning supplies. Both are located in the Dallas, TX area. She is also the founder of the national nonprofit, Cleaning for A Reason, through which she has helped more than 33,000 women with cancer receive free home cleaning.

JM: Hi Debbie, thank you so much for joining me at the campfire. It is such a pleasure to speak with you. You are an incredible leader with a servant's heart. It's safe to say you are a trailblazer when it comes to supporting important causes. Can you explain what exactly cause marketing is to anyone who has not heard of it?

DS: Hi Jon! You bet, so cause marketing is when you use your business and your brand to lift up other social causes in your market. Cause marketing is used when a for-profit business chooses to inject "giving" into their brand. Doing well by doing good, if you will. It's an intentional approach to serving and helping others.

JM: I appreciate your explanation of cause marketing and its significance in today's business landscape. It is creating a win-win situation for both the business and the community it serves. From your perspective, why is it so important in today's day and age?

DS: So differentiation is the hardest part of any service business. Think about it from the customer's perspective. They ask themselves: "Why on earth should I do business with you? Why should I pick you to service my home? Why should I pick your company when given so many choices?" It is so hard to differentiate in a crowded market. I mean, there is a cheap competitor on every corner, and it doesn't matter where you are. We all have low-cost competition. So standing out in a crowded market has become more and more difficult. Everybody has Google reviews and everybody says they're the best. Everybody says they're good at what they do. Everybody says we bring the supplies and all of our work is guaranteed. That's not true differentiation, right? And so many businesses are leading with the lowest common denominator. Most businesses are trying to differentiate themselves by being like everybody, and then they wonder why they're competing on price.

JM: You've raised an important and challenging aspect of running a service business. In a crowded market with low-cost competition, standing out becomes difficult. It's so important to find something that will help a small business stand out amongst the rest. Why is "giving back" so important? Even further, Why should small businesses integrate giving back into their business model?

DS: So a service business that has a mission built into their brand and passion for serving the community helps them stand out in a way their competitors can't stand out. It helps consumers decide if you're the only choice for them versus one of the many choices. We live too much in a world where service businesses have a hard time standing out in the crowd. When your business is one of many, you always compete on price. When your service business stands for important causes, it shines bright. I would say the number one benefit to aligning your brand with giving back is that price is no longer the deciding factor. That's a big deal! I mean, statistics will tell you that 85% of all consumers polled said they would choose a business that's giving back in a meaningful way, even if they're more expensive than the competitor.

JM: I couldn't agree more, integrating giving back into your brand may take time to fully grasp and implement effectively. I can see this has the potential to change the trajectory of a business in so many ways. I loved how you touched on allowing the customers to choose you based on their love for what you do and what you stand for. I love seeing all of the lives your nonprofit has affected by the way. With that said, What's the most rewarding part of your nonprofit's mission?

DS: I would say the most rewarding part is the feeling that I'm truly leading with a heart to serve others. There is nothing like this incredible feeling that you just made someone's day, that you just lifted their spirits or that you just did a good thing with no expectation in return. Here's what I've told entrepreneurs when you own your own business. It's lonely, right? It's lonely being an entrepreneur on the narrow road to success. Your family doesn't really get what you're going through. You can't really talk heart to heart with your employees when you're struggling, and when you're really down or miserable, you certainly can't reveal any of this to your customers. Stepping outside the daily grind of business and embracing giving back brings profound transformation on every level. It shifts your focus to intangible aspects like changing lives and empowers you to become a leader inspiring others to make a difference. When you act with intentionality in your community, people are drawn to follow your example. Employees are motivated to contribute; customers ask how they can be involved. Through leading by example and acting in service, you create a ripple effect, changing not only your own life but also many others. You aren't preaching anything to anyone but rather acting in service, and the result is that you're creating more impact makers. I'm a big believer in teaching people to lift while they climb.

JM: It's truly inspiring to hear about your experiences and the profound impact you've had through your dedication to serving others. I can relate to the fact that serving others has changed me as a business owner. I can also relate to the loneliness of being an entrepreneur. What's a tip you could give to someone who is currently walking the lonely, narrow road?

DS: That embedding a cause into your business, illuminates the path. When you are just thinking about yourself, your customers and the business at hand, things get super hard. When you start thinking about how you can show up for your employees and a worthwhile organization, your paradigm shifts for the better. I feel like this is really the best-kept secret for entrepreneurs. I've worked with a lot of struggling business owners and I hear it all the time: "I'd sure love to give back someday when I'm not struggling. When my business is a little more successful, I'll give back." What they don't understand is that the thought process is rooted in scarcity, not abundance. That right there is one of the reasons they are struggling. That someday I'll have enough to share, but I don't have enough to share today is not true. It's a myth. We all have something to share today. I've come to realize that giving without expectation is literally the path to getting out of scarcity and moving into abundance.

JM: I love that answer! Giving back absolutely illuminates the path to success. What is the reason you decided to start giving back in your business?

DS: I was already giving back in my personal life for a long time. And a lot of people do, especially if you're religious, you give back through your tithe or you have certain pet projects that you give to on a personal level. Here's what I discovered in business though. Corporate giving is 100% different than religious giving of a tithe- 100% different. And so when you give through your religion, you're commanded to give in secret. You're not supposed to give publicly when you're giving to God or giving to your faith, right? But what I discovered is that corporate giving is completely different. If you're a religious person, you're not commanded to give corporately. You're only commanded to give personally. So what I realized is when I give corporately and when I use my business to give back, it typically inspires my competition to step it up and give as well. It puts peer pressure on them to think about using their business for good. I've come to realize that if I just gave in secret, there would be little to no exponential growth. I hear it all the time from customers as well: "How can I participate?"Many of our customers have businesses that they will want to align with yours which is always amazing.

JM: I believe finding the right balance between personal and corporate giving is crucial. When corporate giving is authentic, transparent, and driven by a genuine desire to make a difference, it can not only benefit the causes you support but also enhance your reputation and build a deeper connection with your customers. How would you encourage people to choose what organizations to support?

DS: I came up with the four S's to help guide people. If you use these to guide your decisions, you can hardly make a mistake. So number one, it needs to be *simple*. You have to keep it simple because you are there to run a business before anything. Don't just up and start a nonprofit irrationally. That's a layer of complexity that's destined for failure if you're not ready. You should start by aligning your cause marketing efforts with somebody else's nonprofit. You don't have to reinvent the wheel unless you have the time, the energy and the money for it. Number two. Keep it *safe*. People are easily offended these days so pick a cause that's safe. If you pick political, religious or controversial causes, it's not very safe, and you may find out that half of your customers are offended and run away. Third, it should always be *sincere*. If you don't have a passion for it, it will die out and that's the first clue that it was just a gimmick. You can ask yourself these questions: What truly resonates with you and your heart? What cause do you feel excited about finding ways to either raise money, raise awareness or volunteer with? Then number four, it needs to be *smart* because this strategy is designed to align your brand with a purpose that's long-lasting. Make sure whatever organization you partner with doesn't detract attention away from the service you offer. So I'll give an example of a smart cause because I own a cleaning company and can speak from experience. We partner with a cause that cleans for cancer patients. So it's a very smart and savvy business alignment for us. Whatever trade you're in, make sure it aligns with your cause perfectly.

JM: Thank you for sharing your insight on the four S's. I agree to keep it simple but also carefully consider which organizations you decide to support. I love the example you shared of having your cleaning company partner with a cause that cleans for cancer patients, that is awesome. I admire your success with your business and giving back more than you know, Debbie. I'm curious- How do you define success in business?

DS: I've come to realize that success in business is best defined as time freedom, money freedom, people freedom and purpose freedom. This really helps to make life and business incredibly rich.

Time freedom is having the ability to do whatever you'd like, whenever you'd like to do it.

Money freedom allows you the ability to do those things.

People freedom is the ability to pick and choose who you'd like to do business with (unlike when you first started your business and had to work with anyone just to pay the bills - disrespectful customers, etc). This also applies to employees. When you are free in this area, you don't have to tolerate low level employees. You can replace them with "A Players" who will truly level up your business.

Purpose freedom is the ability to pursue what deeply moves you as an entrepreneur. Giving back and volunteering are examples of a purpose freedom that works for me.

JM: Perfectly said! I just spoke with our mutual friend and industry expert, Brandon Vaughn and asked him: What does it feel like when you reach the top? He said: "Jon, what it really comes down to for me is time freedom- because money is infinite." It's exactly what you just said, just kind of said it in a different fashion, but it's so true. You can always make back money, you can never make back time.

JM: Thank you so much for joining me around the campfire. It was such a pleasure speaking with you Debbie. I do have one last question for you before you go. What advice do you have for someone who is currently climbing their own mountain?

DS: I have two words: start now. Most people postpone their plans, but I believe in taking action. Done is better than perfect. While there may be a perfect way to give back or start a nonprofit, waiting for the perfect time often leads to inaction. As entrepreneurs, we're always busy, and later never comes. If you truly want to begin, start small now. Find a program that resonates with you, your customers, and your employees. Raise funds or volunteer. Starting small now will lead to incredible growth over time. Reflecting back in 10 years, you'll be amazed at the lives you've changed. For anyone who is interested in providing free cleanings to families with cancer, please visit DebbieSardone.com/charity to see how you can support the mission.

The next place to make a tremendous impact sounds simple but believe it or not, most businesses don't do it. This one is all about giving back to your community and to those that need it most. When you are done crafting your team, it's time to move into building your community impact list.

Community:

Begin by creating a list called "Our Community Impact List." This should include nonprofits, charities, foundations and organizations that your company proudly stands behind. Most nonprofits, charities and foundations function to raise funds for specific needs, so these are certainly good fits for you. Organizations cast a wider net and vary from the Chamber of Commerce and Religious Institutions to Firefighter and Police Organizations and more. My best advice is once again to keep it simple as you can always grow and optimize your giving and social impact reach as your business grows and matures. Choose causes that you care about, make sure you find organizations that are legitimate, look for transparency and perform due diligence to make sure they are the real deal. A cool bonus that comes from having a *giving initiative* in place is the fact that it could be a tax write-off. This means that your business is actually rewarded for giving and donating. A very important note when it comes to giving to charities is to make sure this charitable expense is budgeted and accounted for. The key factor in deciding how much your company should donate to charity is your balance sheet — in other words, the amount you budget for philanthropy should be what you can afford to give without affecting the cash flow you need to operate.

Many large corporations and smaller businesses earmark 1% of their pre-tax profit for charitable giving. This isn't a concrete rule though. Some companies give considerably more and others less. Some service businesses choose to donate a percentage of each sale rather than calculate an annualized figure. Here's a note from my past experience. Using a percentage of your profit as a giving guideline makes it easier to scale your donations as your business grows, but it can make it difficult to budget for the year ahead. If you are just rolling out a giving initiative for the first time, keep it as simple as possible.

Once you've established a target amount for your giving, you should do three things to increase the impact of your donation:

1. Make it part of your operating budget.
2. Keep your employees informed and engaged with frequent updates.
3. Make your giving philosophy part of your marketing and outreach strategy.

Something remarkable happens as a business owner when you pivot away from being hyper-focused on only profit as a company. When you start to allocate part of your focus to serving, giving and supporting those in need, everything changes. The changes happen immediately as you write your first check to an organization. Then those good feelings never seem to leave. There's a ripple effect that comes from this. Somehow your employees really take notice of the giving efforts as well.

They started getting super excited about asking clients which organizations they would like to support. They even get excited during the holidays and ask how we can support these organizations even further. This giving effect is contagious, and it really takes on a life of its own.

Then you will go through a moment when all the smoke clears and think about how you made that underprivileged child feel, or that veteran smile, or that less-than-fortunate mother or father light up. You will be given an unshakable feeling of gratitude deep in your heart. Some would even say that's how you do God's work in business.

It's really worth mentioning that you can make a massive impact in your community without donating a portion of your earnings. Say you are just starting out and want to start giving, but money is tight. Drive forward small acts of kindness. Here's what I mean, and I'll use Veterans as an example. Your gift doesn't need to be monetary, it could simply be something from the heart. You can thank a military hero or visit a VA hospital and sit with someone who dedicated their life for us. Whatever it is, I will always push to make an impact on the servicemen and women who selflessly and bravely fight for our freedom and allow us to conduct business.

"Then you will go through a moment when all the smoke clears and think about how you made that underprivileged child feel, or that veteran smile, or that less-than-fortunate mother or father light up, you will be given an unshakable feeling of gratitude deep in your heart. Some would even say that's how you do God's work in business."

Jon Majak

Again, it's easy to put your energy into maximizing your profits. It's hard to be intentional in business. But that's why you are reading this book, because you refuse to be average and don't mind putting in the work that will definitely leave a lasting impression.

How to leave the greatest impact in your community: Call a team meeting and stand up with conviction in your office. Get your team donuts and coffee and pick up your dry-erase marker. Have fun and start asking all of your team members what causes matter to them the most in life. Start putting a list on your whiteboard and engage everyone. Vote for one or a few organizations and be the change you wish to see in the world.

System needed: Assign this responsibility to someone on your team and instruct them to automate the process to the best of their ability. A tip is to set up reminders on your calendar to alert you or one of your employees to touch base with people on your Community Impact List at least two or three times a year. Set up an automatic transfer or post-date a check and ensure it gets out on a given date. Schedule social media posts sharing some of your giving back stories quarterly.

TAKE ACTION:

1. Define how you plan on showing up for your team and the organizations that matter most to you. Who are they and why did you choose them?
2. Post your answer on social media with the hashtags #ringforimpact #ringthebell
3. Visit JonMajak.com/RingTheBell to download and fill out the "Ring the Bell for Impact Document System."

CHAPTER 8:
WHEN YOU RING IT

A s you get off the ground, you rip a straggled piece of your ripped shirt off and walk back over to the bell. You tie the piece of fabric to the top of the bell with one thought in mind, to stake your claim. And boy, did you do just that. You use this moment to be present and think about all of the people who heard and noticed you. Then you smile with gratitude knowing how you could have been even more impactful.

You tell yourself, rather than ring the bell one time for a few minutes straight, I'm going to do it better next time. You create a plan to ring it several times a day and at different times and with different approaches. Your self-talk says: "Today, I'm going to ring it at the break of dawn with both hands. Later, I'm going to preserve my energy and ring it with just my left hand. Then tonight, I'll make the town notice me while ringing it with my right hand." Against all odds, you've found out the key to getting noticed is frequency, consistency and timing.

🔔

The time is right now, but you have to be ready. The companies that are the most proactive in their marketing efforts are the ones who always come out on top. Your marketing, admin and sales systems must be on point, and you must have the capacity to fulfill the flood of new work orders. You don't have to have every answer or have a perfect business by any means, but you must be ready to handle an influx of new business.

You need to be able to look at your business from an aerial snapshot at this point. You must be able to step back and out of the business to really see the trends of when you have leads pouring in and when they start to dry up. As Donald Trump says: "Opportunities are never lost, just found by those who clearly see the power of trends and timing." When you can see this vision clear in your mind, things start to get exciting. You will be able to see the ebbs and flows of sales within your business. The key here is to make sure you have a solid grip on the peaks and valleys that exist in your operation.

"The companies that are the most proactive in their marketing efforts are the ones who always come out on top."

Jon Majak

Most home service businesses have to take into account when a season starts and when it ends. That's why there is so much power in knowing when your sales historically and predictably start to trend downward so that you can have measures in place to stop that dip. I don't want you to only stop the plunge but instead create methods to turn those weaker performing months into strong and prosperous months.

If you've been at the game of business for a long time, you most likely know in your gut when things slow down and when they ramp up, but a breakthrough happens when you actually see the data visually. You instantly become a more effective marketer and can leverage the metrics to help you understand when the best time is to deploy certain growth engines.

When do you actually ring the bell? The direct answer is you should always be making noise and strive to be heard. What does that actually mean in terms of execution? It means that once a year, you build out your marketing calendar, set it in motion and be heard throughout the year! Just be mindful that it's a living document that gets regularly modified based on lead-flow, demand and capacity. That's why the most important component of "When to Ring the Bell" is your Marketing Calendar. A marketing calendar is a plan that covers your marketing activities for the entire year. It's essential because you need to know when to precisely launch your most effective growth engines.

"Opportunities are never lost, just found by those who clearly see the power of trends and timing."

Donald Trump

The impact component of this book is also directly related to your marketing calendar. When you embed scheduled "giving" into the calendar, your Community Impact List will come to life. What ultimately happens is you end up creating a deeper and more meaningful marketing calendar (Call it your Marketing Calendar 2.0)

Your Marketing Calendar can be as simple or complex as you'd like to make them. Keep it simple.

I'm keeping this chapter short and here's why. Like I promised you, I'm giving you zero fluff and all value. The value-add from this chapter is coming from an implementation video that will help you step by step. This will be everything you need to hit the ground running. Once you have the calendar created to make the most money possible, start adding in your scheduled giving into the calendar. Don't overthink it. The name of the game is to just make sure you aren't winging or giving sporadically. Give intentionally and know in advance when it's time to do so.

Campfire Chat with Expert Mountain Climber:

Michael Grigery, CEO of Click Call Sell

About Michael:

As a father, husband, CEO of Click Call Sell and CONQUER Coach, Michael spends his days working in the trenches with small business owners, leading a team of marketing experts and his nights chasing around an energetic toddler. He's a servant leader and loves to over-deliver and share all the expert advice and experience he's gained over the past 10 years of being surrounded by the best and brightest in the home service space.

JM: Hi Michael! Thank you for joining me at the campfire. It is such a pleasure to sit and chat, I have yet to see anyone explain marketing calendars in the home service industry better than you. What's the best advice you can give someone that's looking to market their business with laser-targeted precision?

MG: Identify your service area & hot spots: One of my favorite reports to analyze is revenue and work orders by zip code. It's almost certain that 99% of home service businesses will service 50 or more zip codes in a calendar year yet 50% of their revenue is coming from 5 or less zip codes. Focus on the 5, not the 50.

When you market to a targeted area, you're effectively maximizing penetration rates, brand awareness and referrals while increasing routing efficiency and profitability.

Stay laser-focused on niche: As the CEO and visionary of your company, you have a seemingly limitless potential to offer any service at any time. A service offering that is too narrow can slow growth, or worse, can create opportunities for competition to steal your clients. A service offering that is too broad is difficult to train, causes logistics challenges and can make marketing confusing when a company is trying to be all things to all people.

There's a comprehensive strategy behind why your industry influencers and national franchise brands create service offerings. Craft your service offering to be a list of complimentary services that are high frequency / low price and low frequency / high price. A great example I like to use is with landscaping.

Mowing lawns isn't exactly sexy, but it's also the #1 exterior home service. As the perfect high frequency / low price service, a landscaping company can also offer seeding, spraying, mulch, aeration, turf installation, softscapes, hardscapes or any exterior lawn/tree service to build a database and remarket to them forever. If you have 1,000 low-ticket clients and can sell 1% of them a high-ticket item, you're a 7-figure company.

Track seasonality and anticipate demand: You can't spend your way out of a slump. When demand is low, focus on marketing to your existing database and larger commercial jobs. Demand is low for a reason. Trying to change consumer buying habits is expensive.

When putting together your marketing calendar, focus on the acronym; A.C.E.

A: Anticipate - The #1 challenge for most home service companies is getting to capacity. In a seasonal business, the person who can get to capacity the fastest usually wins. Set your marketing up so that you can go from 0 - 100 as fast as possible. That means having your trucks, techs and marketing all ready to go once the season/weather breaks.

C: Capitalize - Strike while the iron is hot. When demand is high, everything works. Once you hit capacity, be thoughtful with your marketing spending, focusing on what you're most confident will keep your schedule full. During peak season, leads are the most affordable. If you're at capacity before the season starts, you can actually reduce your spending due to the low cost of leads.

E: Extend - To extend the season means knowing your company's seasonality and aggressively marketing at the end of the season. Your goal should be to be booked out farther the last week of your season than at any point during the year. I'd suggest looking at your historical demand, going back 3-4 weeks from there and being as aggressive with your marketing as possible during this time. The goal here is to mitigate the decreased demand during the slower months.

Craft unique messaging based on where your client is in the buying cycle: What grabs attention depends on where your customers are in the buying cycle. I'm not sure about you, but I've never logged onto Facebook or TikTok thinking, "oh boy, I really hope a painting company shows me an ad today."

Lead generation all starts with awareness. Awareness comes in two parts.

Awareness of your brand: The customer knows your brand exists.

Awareness of your service offering: The customer knows you offer the service.

Capturing demand is significantly cheaper than creating demand. If you're trying to educate a market that a service exists, you're going to have a harder time than marketing your brand as an option for the service.

Creating interest in your brand/service offering is the most common way to market to the masses and drive significant lead flow. These are customers that most likely know the service you offer exists but aren't actively thinking about it. Your job as the marketer is to convince them that they need you. This messaging is typically based on a pattern interrupt, urgency/scarcity or limited-time offering. Some examples of marketing channels to create interest are direct mail, social media or boots on the ground. What makes the interest phase special is its unique ability to market to a seemingly endless audience. Anyone in your service area who's a target client can see your ads and become a client.

Finally, the holy grail of marketing is the decision and action phase of the buying cycle. These are the customers who are going to Google, Bing Angie's List or asking their friends for recommendations. They're probably ready to make a decision on what and when to buy. Converting these customers is more about how much trust and credibility you can create through your messaging. This is why branding, reviews and a professional website are so important. Your job with bottom-of-funnel clients is to create enough trust and credibility to make the customer believe you can solve their problem.

JM: This is some great insight, thank you for sharing all this info. For most service entrepreneurs, understanding how and when to market their business can be overwhelming. What's the easiest way to explain to someone how to use a marketing calendar using data and not their gut?

MG: The marketing calendar is the single most important tool you can use to control growth. Owning a service company is hard. Marketing is one small part of running your business, and without proper planning, it can get overlooked or forgotten. Without a lead generation plan, it's easy to become reactive. When you're reacting to the season, it reduces your ability to control growth and maximize lead costs.

A marketing calendar is a living document that is regularly modified based on lead flow, demand and capacity. When building your marketing calendar, follow these steps:

Start with your existing database. I like to reserve 1% of my sales goal for marketing to my current customers and referral gifts. You should be in frequent contact with your current customers through phone, email and snail mail. Remember to anticipate your season, starting 2-3 weeks early. Then extend the season by pushing again 2-3 weeks before the demand season slows.

Next, move to your proven channels. What do you know works,

and how much can you spend before reaching a point of diminishing returns? The best money is spent right when demand hits and will be a primary contributor in your race to capacity. Start at the bottom of the funnel and work your way up. Remember that capturing demand is much more economical than creating demand. Focus your efforts on where people are looking and when they're looking. And remember, you can't spend your way out of a slump. Focus most of your effort on the beginning and end of each season.

Moving up the funnel, work on branding initiatives (Facebook, Social Media, Direct Mail, etc). There is a direct correlation between brand impressions and conversion rates. The more people that know your brand, the more leads you're going to get. Branding campaigns help people search for you specifically rather than an industry term. From our research, you're 5 times more likely to close a deal when a consumer searches for a brand term vs. an industry term.

Networking & Boots on the Ground (BOG) tactics: The benefit of BOG marketing is it typically takes more of a time commitment than a financial one. A big miss I see a lot of home service companies make is forgetting what got them to grow. Once most businesses get traction, they lose focus on what got them there. In most cases, BOG marketing was a huge contributor to their success.

Estimating & Sales Materials: Make sure you save the budget for your branded sales materials, including estimate packs, service brochures, business cards, etc.

Experimenting: If you have extra budget and want to try something new, always test when demand is at its peak. If people aren't buying when everyone else is buying, you either have bad media or a bad offer.

JM: You bring up a crucial point about the significance of a marketing calendar in managing and controlling the growth of a service company. Without a solid lead generation plan, businesses often find themselves in a reactive mode, constantly scrambling to adapt to seasonal fluctuations or market trends. Is there a very simple marketing calendar formula for someone to follow?

MG: Check out JonMajak.com/RingTheBell

JM: You've got an impressive background in both franchise and small business service companies. What tactics should small businesses learn from the big players?

MG: When I started my career as a franchisee in 2010, I honestly thought there was no way a small, non-franchised business could possibly compete with a well-run franchise organization. As I became more familiar with different franchise organizations, I started to realize that not all franchises are created equal. Some are incredible, while others fall well short of any basic expectations of a brand in a box.

In 2016, I met Josh Latimer who would change my perspective on small, non-franchised businesses forever. His online training courses were audio gold. For the first time, I saw a blueprint for success that wasn't packaged as a franchise. In fact, what Josh was doing in 2016 was the beginning of a home service business renaissance. Today, there are more coaching programs and options than ever before. People who don't want to buy into a franchise have an equal opportunity for success.

I do believe there is and always will be a place for franchise organizations. Building a respectable brand from nothing is incredibly difficult. For people who don't want to start from scratch, a franchise is a fantastic option. Be careful when selecting a franchise. There are equally amazing and terrible organizations. Do your due diligence!

JM: Thank you for all this great insight, Michael. Thank you for taking the time to sit down at the campfire with me. One last question for you, What's the best advice you can give someone who's currently climbing their own mountain?

MG: Believe in yourself and know that you are capable of greatness. By having a goal, writing it down, taking action and even reading this book, you've done more than most ever will. There are a couple items that keep me going on my entrepreneurial journey.

Tony Robbins says that your level of success is in direct proportion to the amount of uncertainty you can handle. Take big chances and believe in your abilities. The bigger you think, the bigger you'll be.

You will inevitably hit the ceiling. Be aware of your individual strengths, always practice leadership and never stop learning. Your ability to lead and influence others to help bring your vision to life is what separates ordinary and extraordinary.

🔔

Before you drive forward your marketing calendar too fast, it's important we cover some basic marketing terms. The first is called your CPL or your Cost Per Lead. Understanding how much you pay dollar for dollar for a lead from a certain lead source is crucial when it comes to growing and scaling your business.

The next important term to know is called your CPA or your Cost Per Acquisition. Essentially, this is a marketing metric that measures the total cost to acquire a single paying customer for your business.

The third really important term you need to know is called your CAC or your Customer Acquisition Cost. Customer acquisition cost (CAC) is the cost related to acquiring a new customer.

The final term I want you to have a good understanding of is one we touched on earlier in the book and that is the LTV or the lifetime value. This is how much you'll make off a given customer over the lifetime of your business. The reason it's so crucial to have your eye on LTV is because, in certain businesses, it's not all about getting an immediate ROI. Businesses that have a recurring revenue model such as landscapers, might not make their money back until their fifth month of service. However, when they make it back, it's a huge win because that account is now profitable for the rest of the customer's journey with your business. On the contrary, companies like pool builders, which is a one-off service, must make their money back immediately. If they spend $5000 a month and only yield one small job of $4000, they lost $1,000 and have little to no opportunity to make up for the lost revenue in the future from this customer.

Now that you have the groundwork laid, you must understand the importance of measuring your return on investment. When you go through the process of tracking your ROI, you must never lump all of your marketing activities together against the amount you spent. Instead, you must get granular and measure your return for each lead source or growth engine specifically. For example, if you spent $2000 a month on Facebook Ads and received 125 leads, your average cost per lead is $16. If you spent $2000 a month on those Facebook Ads and closed $10,000 in new business, then you got a 5 to 1 return, and that's a fair ROI.

As you know by now, I'm a huge believer in keeping things simple, so I'm not going to break down every detail on how to build out the calendar in this book. Instead, I've created a place to watch a simple "how to" video on how to easily create one. You can find it at JonMajak.com/RingTheBell. So you can know what to expect, here are the 5 steps covered in the video.

Step 1: Priming your mindset

Step 2: Leveraging your past data

Step 3: Timing is everything

Step 4: Automate & Delegate

Step 5: Test

TAKE ACTION:

1. Visit JonMajak.com/RingTheBell to watch the "How to Create a Marketing Calendar" video and fill out the "Marketing Calendar" Worksheet.

CHAPTER 9:
PROTECT THE BELL

T
he entire town wants to know more about the man on top of the mountain. You can feel the energy that people want to meet you. But before you trek back down to introduce yourself with a smile, you focus on one instinctive thing- protecting the bell. You walk over to it and offer it a moment of pure appreciation. You even fall to your knees and pray with gratitude. You also know that the moment that you make your way back down the mountain, that other people will want to visit and ring the bell themselves.

So before you head down, you pull out a piece of paper and a pen from your backpack. You write a script for the next visitor. You talk about who you are, why you rang the bell and what you hope to get out of it. You end the note with:

"Whenever you're done ringing the bell, make sure to leave your mark up here in hopes it will help the next climber. Create a script, leave a note or just simply tell others the importance of climbing to the top of their own mountains in life. Help others every chance you get."

-Carpe Diem

🔔

You must Protect the Bell. What does this mean? Protecting the Bell simply means that you were absolutely relentless in ringing the bell to drum up business and change lives, and now you will do whatever it takes to maintain your hard-earned success for life. By far, the most important advice I could offer when it comes to protecting the bell, starts with you. Working your way through the narrow road and up the largest mountain of your life took a lot out of you. Now, you must protect your mental, physical and spiritual health. If your mind is not as sharp as a tack and you aren't taking care of it proactively, it's only a matter of time until life catches up to you and pulls you away from the bell. If your physical health isn't at its peak level, you will always be playing catch-up rather than leading the pack. I'm also convinced that we are all spiritual beings having a human experience. That being said, if you don't practice some sort of soul care on yourself, such as meditating, practicing gratitude, reading scripture, plugging into positive audio such as inspirational podcasts or audiobooks, reading etc. you will succumb to the struggles life throws at you in time. It doesn't matter how hard you hold onto that rope or how tight you hug that big beautiful bell. If you don't continuously take measures to boost your well-being and grow, you don't stand a chance at staying on top long-term.

Pausing to reflect and look inside my backpack: Here's a quick look into my morning routine and the importance of creating your own.

I have a morning routine that I follow every day of my life to the best of my ability. If for some reason it doesn't get done, my day is never as strong as it should be. Seven days a week, I wake up early before the sun rises, and tell myself 5 things that I'm grateful for. I then drink a large cup of water and do some sort of physical exercise to drive my body forward. Then I make sure to be very intentional about strengthening my mind. I meditate, pray, and listen to some sort of inspirational audio. Next, I visualize my life and business goals. I look at my vision board and read over a commitment letter that I write to myself at the beginning of every year. That letter talks about what I must accomplish that year, and I also signed it when I made the commitment. Finally, I take a shower and get after my day. This is my routine and it works for me, but you must do what's best for you. Feel free to replicate or modify.

The next thing you need to be aware of is the importance of educating yourself. Always be learning. Albert Einstein once said: "Once you stop learning, you start dying." Stay a student of this entrepreneurial game for as long as you can. Whatever field of work you are in, be relentless at staying ahead of the curve and keeping a mindset of always innovating. Visit shops and offices of businesses that are steps ahead of you. Be a sponge and work on replicating their successful systems. The most powerful CEOs I know have a servant-leader mindset and would be willing to show you whatever you need to help you succeed.

Read as many books as you can and do your best to make it to the trade shows and conventions where you can grow relationships, learn more and plant seeds to grow your wealth. I strongly recommend looking into consulting and business coaching as well. But it's extremely important that you hire a consultant or coach that has already walked in your shoes and/or has the assassin-like skills to scale small businesses like it's nobody's business. There's too many smoke and mirror coaching programs out there that will take you to the cleaners. Open your eyes, ask questions and if you start to sniff out a phony, run far away. On the flip side, if you come across a home run hitting program and your intuition is telling you this will help you level up, put the throttle down and go. If you are lucky enough to link up with the right coaches and mentors, you will dramatically fast forward your success.

I was lucky enough to have a mentor in my life for as long as I could remember. His name is Brandon Rosen, and we've been friends since childhood. He is the definition of someone who rang the bell to the best of his ability. His companies have generated hundreds of millions of dollars and have made such a major impact on so many lives. It's an honor to call him one of my best friends, and watching him change the world amazes me. It's hard to name people who would drop anything for you to see you succeed so you can join them at the table. He is that friend, and I am forever grateful. Take a minute and think about who that person is to you and let them know. People like this don't want gifts or money from you, the greatest way to thank them is to win and let them know how intricate of a role they played in your success. Get yourself a mentor and or a coach sooner than later. The future you will be grateful you did.

"If your mind is not as sharp as a tack and you aren't taking care of it proactively, it's only a matter of time until life catches up to you and pulls you away from the bell."

Jon Majak

Another way to protect the bell is to make sure that you spin more than one basket. It's essential that you stay laser-focused on the business that is your self-mined diamond, but you must diversify as you grow in your journey. I'm not necessarily saying start more and more businesses, but I am saying make sure you have your money working for you in more ways than one. If you choose to add more service offerings to your company, that achieves it. If you choose to start another business, that achieves it. If you choose to invest in other areas, that achieves it. I'm certainly no financial advisor, but something huge happens when you get away from the mindset of just having your savings grow on a slow build. It feels really good when your money is spread out over a bunch of different areas, and each one of those areas is exponentially growing and creating wealth for you. They don't teach you this in school. Well that's not technically one hundred percent true. You can learn all of this in the school of hard knocks, as I did. You might trip and stumble more than the next guy, but you'll get there.

That's all that truly matters in the end.

Protecting the bell is also all about protecting and keeping the customers you've worked so hard to acquire. That's why having a solid handle on your customer life cycle and mapping out each step of their journey within your business is paramount. Truthfully, earning their business one time isn't that major of an accomplishment if you sell low-ticket offerings. If you sell high tickets, such as a new roof or new HVAC system, that's a different story. The real challenge is retaining that business and turning those customers into loyal, raving fans for life. So it begs the question- what can you do to make sure you keep your perfect customers in your life for good? It's all about nurturing your customer list, aka your database, like never before. You must fight tooth and nail to show your customers love, be on time, do what you say you're going to do, offer excellent service, provide incredible value, and be relationship driven. I promise you this- if you don't, your competition will.

How do you stay in touch with your customers? You must have a great CRM (Customer Relationship Management) software that you are able to input detailed notes in about every account you service. During your relationship with them, discover where they are from, what their hobbies are, what they do for work, what they do for fun, and keep excellent tabs for your records. Some people might think that's a little much but not me. I've made a ton of money being hyper-focused on the small details most avoid. When it's all said and done, make sure you get in front of them through follow-up sequences such as phone calls, text messages, email blasts, ringless voicemails, direct mail etc. Another really strategic way to put focus into retention is to get your customers to like and follow your business on Facebook and Social Media. It will take some effort to make this happen, but because you operate at an excellent level, I'm sure that's no big deal! So when you get your customers to like your page, you are essentially getting them to "buy in" and join your extended family. When you get a couple hundred real, satisfied customers to follow your business page, you have essentially created the most targeted audience possible.

Now imagine if you could turn those two hundred followers into twenty-two thousand customers or more over the years. Now you're cooking with some real heat. You can then officially spoon-feed direct messages and specials to your loyal following, leading to more and more business. The name of the game is to figure out how to acquire as many perfect customers as possible and then keep them in your fold for as long as possible.

"Once you stop learning, you start dying."
Albert Einstein

We can't talk about totally protecting your success without touching on the importance of staying ahead of the curve in business. Marketing strategies and advertising are changing by the day, and what worked last year, might not have any relevance in today's market. Think about how much artificial intelligence aka AI has changed the game in such a short time. With that said, keep your finger on the pulse of innovation. In fact, work towards blazing the trail yourself. Where do I think marketing is heading? I truly believe that there will always be a fundamental need for advertisements both on and off line. I also believe that we are headed in a very different experiential and augmented reality-driven world. I believe that placing the customer at the forefront of all decisions in business is the future. Amazon founder, Jeff Bezos said: "The number one thing that has made us successful by far is obsessive-compulsive focus on the customer." I believe that experiences are going to play a major role in high-level marketing as life progresses.

Think about how large corporations have already adopted and implemented experiential marketing in so many ways. Companies like DoorDash and Instacart don't just drop off food and leave. They mapped out the entire customer journey to the tee and hit the bullseye doing so. They have "easy to use" apps with "best in class" products that are simply just added to the checkout cart. Then you can watch the entire process unfold through the app and eventually receive your goods without any question of when they will reach your doorstep. Then it's all tied up with a bow by being able to rate your service post delivery. It's absolutely incredible when you really think about it!

I gave you that example on purpose. We have all ordered food in our lifetime, and we all have an idea of what that experience looks and feels like. Now apply the same strategy to the home service business if you would.

Imagine if Mrs. Jones orders a roof cleaning service. The days of old were all about fulfilling the order and collecting payment. In the future, I believe that the experience will be on another level. We will either be at a point where a technician will be walking on the roof and talking about the preparation, application and cleanup processes as they are actually cleaning, or there will be a drone cleaning the roof, and the operator will be offering a voiceover experience on how the process is going and offer an estimated time of completion as the service progresses. The recording will then be saved to an app or the cloud, where Mrs. Jones can access it at any moment for various reasons. The contract will be created through a Non Fungible Token, aka NFT, and the transaction will be handled automatically, and so will the review and/or recommendation request.

I believe that this experiential marketing will apply to any and all home service businesses. Whether you're in the HVAC, Pool, Christmas Lighting, Gutter, Roofing or any other service business- you must think about leveling up the experience you offer. Don't overthink it. Start making some small changes today so you are ahead of the curve.

There is power in imperfect action! Start texting Mrs. Jones that your crew is on the way. Start setting up some cameras while you service the property. (You can use this raw media in your marketing as standard pictures, video, or time-lapsed video. You can also send this to the customer, so they can feel involved in the process.) Start informing the customer in three phases- when you've arrived, how the job is going at the halfway point, and when it's complete. Start handling all your transactions digitally. Start automating your review generation experience. Start by re-engaging the satisfied customer for more work or referrals through text, email and ringless voicemail follow-up sequences. Get AI involved in every single way possible. There are so many resources popping up daily on how AI will support your efforts. I could probably write a whole book on just how powerful and useful AI is for your service business. Just take it from me, start leveraging wherever and whenever you can. By making these small tweaks right now, you are literally taking measures to protect the bell and outpace the competition.

Remember, the only thing that's constant in life is change. If you would've asked people 50 years ago that we would have every answer imaginable to every question we have in a smart little rectangular box that we put in our pocket, people would think you were crazy. Never underestimate innovation and the power of creative thinking and execution!

Campfire Chat with Expert Mountain Climber:

Curt Kempton, Founder of ResponsiBid

About Curt:

Curt Kempton is the Founder and CEO of Symphosize, LLC, where he has developed a service quoting software known as ResponsiBid and provides consulting to service businesses. In this role, Curt manages the creative, development, sales, and support teams. Prior to starting his software & consulting business, he graduated in 2005 from ASU's business school as the "outstanding graduating student of his class" while simultaneously managing a bike shop for 5 years, paying his way through college. After graduating from ASU, Curt started and ran his pressure washing and window cleaning company for 7 years before selling it in 2014 to do ResponsiBid full-time.

JM: Hey Curt! So glad to have you here around the campfire. I admire your experience and would love to hear your perspective on a few things. It's all about keeping customer experience at the forefront of business in today's world. Why is it so important for Home Service Companies to deliver an exceptional experience in this day and age?

CK: Hi Jon, pleasure to spend time with you! First, an excellent experience serves the customer at the highest level. Additionally, because your employees are the ones actively engaging in the front lines on a daily basis, it serves them at a very high level as well. The legacy that you're building is the customer journey that you put your customers through. But when you bring in the dimension of it being in this day and age, customers behave differently now than they did 10 years ago. Nowadays, customers have a lot less patience for getting to where they're trying to go. Point A to Point B is very important. The journey is essentially this: "I am curious about x. And I'm not sure if I'm going to do anything at point y, right? Like, how much is the cost? Who's going to come? What's going to happen when they do the work? Will they meet my needs? Is it a good value?" In this new age customers want assurances, they want reviews, they want quick answers to their questions. The idea is that your business has a certain DNA, and you must weave that into what the customer was expecting. That DNA ends up being on permanent display.

JM: I love that you touched on the new fast-paced world, where technology has transformed consumer behaviors and created a desire for instant gratification. It's crucial to embrace a mindset of adaptation rather than getting stuck in old ways. Customers now want their inquiries addressed quickly and their concerns attended to with care. By putting a major emphasis on being great at following up, Home Service

Pros can meet these evolving customer needs head-on. In your opinion, Why should Home Service Pros put a major emphasis on being great at following up?

CK: From a macro standpoint, excellent follow-up is the differentiation between a business that is in business to serve their clients, as opposed to a business that is in business to serve themselves. A lot of entrepreneurs start off in the wrong mindset because they're trying to replace a paycheck, and their business exists for them. So many people focus so much on what's in it for them, and taking the time to follow up with the customers or tell them something that's useful can simply get in the way of them earning their paycheck in their mind. Most business owners don't even intentionally take into account all of the sacrifices the homeowner has to make to even do business with them. Whether it's taking time away from work, figuring out how to verbalize what they want done because it's not their field of expertise or countless other reasons, the customer has skin in the game too. You can't go wrong by centering back to making sure you create the most beautiful customer journey possible.

JM: I always say: "stop selling and start helping." By prioritizing customer needs and ensuring their satisfaction, you can create a strong foundation of trust, leading to increased business, referrals, and positive reviews. In today's world where technology is a staple, it is pretty crucial for any business's success. It's also important for companies to forward think on every level. Why should home service providers leverage technology in their business?

CK: It's so important that we give people what they expect. Nowadays, we're all carrying phones that have more technology in them than the first spaceship to the moon had. That's crazy to think about! But the fact is, that it used to be that if you're a hard-working, good old boy, your business would grow, and relationships would build. In today's day and age, labor is way too expensive, automations are very inexpensive, technology is too fundamental, and quite frankly, it never sleeps. I like to say, look at your own life and think about how important technology is to you. That's how important it is to your customer. If you're still doing your appointments on a handwritten book, you're missing out on the efficiencies and your customer is missing out on the excellent experience that comes from technology. The fact is that you simply cannot run an intimate business, not at the level that's required anymore to keep a business humming at scale without technology.

JM: Understanding the importance of technology to our own lives helps us realize its significance to our customers. Embracing technology, whether it's using digital tools for appointments or leveraging communication channels, enhances efficiency and provides an excellent customer experience. Let's talk about the power of your software and how it's improving sales for Home Service Pros. Why does automated bidding software like ResponsiBid consistently boost average ticket prices compared to the old-school sales approach?

CK: The idea of ResponsiBid is that we want to close more jobs on average, at higher average ticket prices, with less effort than the old-school way. As far as the formula goes, the old way was to give your customer an ultimatum. Think about it as if you were running a carpet cleaning business. Mrs. Jones would call the company to get a free estimate, and the business owner would typically say: "My price is $350." Without really being mindful of it, that puts the customer in a really tough position. The problem is that you, as the expert, are probably thinking about several other things that aren't communicated, such as our carpet cleaning is much better because it goes deeper with steam and enzymes, and we metabolize the oils, so stains don't return. Or we do this process that makes it so that it'll dry really fast, or all these different value propositions that you, as the expert, just take for granted that you know, and your customer is sort of forced to look at the price as the main event. So clean carpets for $350, or clean carpets from your competitor for $200. Well, in that situation, your customer would be foolish to choose you, because they're comparing what they think is the same thing for two very wildly different prices. So the reason that we can close a higher average number of people at higher average ticket prices, is because it's about not giving them an ultimatum, we don't just give one price. It's either Option A, Option B or Option C. Our approach involves providing multiple options: Good, Better, and Best, each with increasing value and customer satisfaction. For example, the Good option offers basic carpet cleaning, while the Better option includes additional services like carpet protection and upholstery cleaning. The best option goes even further, encompassing tile cleaning, grout coloration, and sealing. By bundling services and creating a curated customer experience, we have seen significant increases in average ticket prices. 'Yes or No' is a very lonely place. But when you say do you want this, this or that? And the value is standing right out in front of me- I move from research mode into decision mode much quicker. Since we rolled out bundling, I thought people were going to see a large increase in their average ticket price, and it would end there. I was actually hopeful that they would be doubling their average ticket price. More often than not, I'm hearing people quadrupling their average ticket price.

JM: Wow, that's incredible that you are able to help business owners often double, triple or quadruple their average ticket prices. I really appreciate you sharing this and sharing the benefit of giving the customers 3 options to choose from. I know there is a lot of change with how customers are buying and a lot of changes happening with technology as well. What does the future of software and technology in the home service industry look like, in your opinion?

CK: It's great to see the transformation that's happening for future generations in the service industry. Amazon is changing a lot of things and helping people love the technology experience. I believe that what's going to happen is that business owners are going to walk into a room with their phone or smart device, and the technology will go to work. Similar to facial recognition, a smart device will get a map of your whole house, and I believe that you'll walk into a room, and you'll get a 360 view with the LIDAR mapping out your whole house. It will be able to tell how thick your walls are. It will be able to tell what kind of windows you have. It will be able to tell how many square feet the room is. It will know how tall the ceilings are. It will literally map everything. You can do it in every single room in your house. And you'll have a file, and you're going to use that file in so many different ways. I believe you'll be able to upload it to obtain all sorts of different home services. If you want your walls painted, you upload the LIDAR map of your house, and the paint technicians are going to use that map in a format that is sort of standardized. You'll just take that file, and your home painter will know exactly how many square feet of trim you've got, how many square feet of wall you have, how many linear feet of cuttings need to be made. I think that's going to go all the way into your plumbing, window replacements, roof cleaning, maid service and every other vertical within the service industry. I honestly don't think we've even scratched the surface of what LIDAR is going to be able to do.

JM: Reflecting back on how far technology has come is mind blowing and it is even crazier to think where it will be in a couple of years considering the recent explosion of AI. Technology has significantly advanced for home service business owners over the years, that's for sure. It's safe to say that ResponsiBid has changed the game by flipping the paradigm from buying "services" to buying "products" that you essentially add to cart, if you will. So that leads me to my next question- Why should Home Service Pros consider productizing their service offerings?

CK: Products are pretty easy to buy because they're physical, and you can typically hold and touch them. The reason is that psychologically, it's easier for a human who can touch and feel something and sort of move that feeling to the emotional part of their brain really quick and easy. The idea of clean carpets, clean toilets or a pressure-washed house can appear hard to productize. But when it's done right, it's so worth it. This discovery allows you to move to another bigger and more incredible dimension in business. When any purchases are made, we do our best as humans to keep it logical, until we can't anymore. Then we eventually make the emotional decision and move forward. So in research mode, the brain goes like this, you're going to buy something on Amazon, in research mode, you're reading reviews, you're trying to figure out what the specifications of the thing are that you're buying, will it meet your needs. And then, at some point, there's a switch that flips into decision mode, we go from research to decision, and it happens in about an instant, you just go, I think I'll just go with that. And the reason that that happens is because your brain feels like logically, you've jumped through all the hoops that it needs to in order to feel like it's in control of the situation, you're not being taken advantage of. You're not wasting resources, and the problem that you're solving is definitely worth buying the thing. Well, if someone's buying clean windows, they're trying to buy an emotional result. Zero into that and allow your productized service to deliver that feeling to them. Productizing the Good, Better, Best options will allow people to move from research mode to decision mode very quickly, because I'm buying a solution to an actual problem, as opposed to just a simple one-off service.

JM: The points you raised about the psychological aspect of purchasing products versus services are super insightful. When someone seeks clean windows, they are ultimately pursuing an emotional outcome. By zeroing in on that emotional connection and delivering it through productized services, that can transition customers from research to decision mode quickly. Thank you so much for taking time to sit with me at the campfire. I have one last question for you Curt, What advice do you have for someone who's currently climbing their own mountain?

CK: It's crazy because our family logo is about climbing your mountain. I'm a big believer that we all must work towards climbing to the top whenever we can. If we're talking about a business owner that has a vision of what they're trying to accomplish, the first thing is, you've got to make it through "The Narrow Road." Then take steps every day towards progress. You need to know what that looks like and have a clear vision. You can't tell yourself, I want to be there one day and keep your fingers crossed. You must write down two or three things that you can do to get closer to that mountain top and then execute like never before!

🔔

Now, let's continue to discuss how we'll protect the bell. When you arrive and start making money and creating an impact in life, people really start to notice you. In this mix of people, competitors start to show up in your life more than ever. You will get a lot of inbound phone calls from people pretending they are customers when they are nothing more than snipers trying to poach everything they can from you so they can also become successful. The question is: how do you handle it? It's simple. Do not get defensive and push competitors away. My advice is actually the complete opposite, and that is to embrace competition. Be humble and stay humble always. It will get you much farther than you think. Let others in your service area badmouth your competition. But not you. It's not how you are built. You don't need to throw dirt on someone else's name to get ahead in business. They say a rising tide raises all ships so help others whenever you get the opportunity.

I have a reason why I love competition so much. There was a time when I was building my service business, that we became so busy that we couldn't handle any more work. We had so many trucks on the road and were maxed out in capacity but the calls were still flowing in. I decided to start selling leads and also subcontracting work out. One day, I saw one of my competitors wearing his company shirt while he was out at breakfast with his family. I remember thinking, he seems like a nice guy and maybe I can give him some of my overflow work. I didn't want to bother him while he was enjoying his family time but I did make a mental note of his company name. The following week, the calls were raining in like crazy and he came to mind. I Googled his company and gave him a call to introduce myself and asked him if he'd ever like to take on some extra work. His name was Dan and I loved his vibe and we bonded instantly. Dan had an abundance mindset as well and said he'd be grateful for any additional work I could throw his way.

The beautiful part about this story is we made a ton of money together and we built a genuine friendship over the years. When it finally came time to hang up my pressure washing gun and complete my journey in the business, I decided to put the company up for sale on the market. Guess who ended up buying my business? The "competitor" who I became good friends with and made a lot of money with along the way. I was secure in my journey and so was he, therefore, we were able to build a relationship established on trust and a genuine respect for each other. He took over my business and has acquired several other businesses since then. He is now known as the busiest pressure washing company in South Florida, if not all of Florida. It makes me smile when I think about how well he is doing and how far he's come. I rang the bell and it impacted him years ago, and watching him take things to the next level impacts me in so many ways. I love it. The moral of the story is to embrace your competition and lift each other up whenever the opportunity arises.

When you create alliances in your local market, you are building out your network. I've said it my whole life but I'm a firm believer that when you increase your network, you increase your net worth. If you ever have the chance to be over 150% capacity and you are turning away a ton of jobs, build the right relationships with your competition and give them your overflow work for a percentage. Additionally, you will also have a safe place to bounce both good and bad ideas off of other local leaders with similar businesses and create some amazing friendships along the way. So when you see competition running up the hill, eyeing to get their swing on the bell, encourage them to do so and let them know you got their back. Always be living and operating with an abundance mindset, not one of scarcity and life will fall into place for you. Just never forget that you are the champion and you came to win, not come in second. So help others whenever you can but always, I mean *always*, stay gunning for the championship ring and rose celebration.

I wouldn't be helping you protect everything if I didn't mention the importance of protecting your money. You literally just learned how to make the most money possible in this business. Now you must fight to keep it and ensure it's always growing. The first thing you need to do is make sure your business is operating in the right ranges. For example, are your Cost of Goods Sold in the right ranges? Are you spending too much on labor or supplies? Knowing where you need to be so you aren't bleeding money is crucial in the pursuit of protection.

Campfire Chat with Expert Mountain Climber:

Meaghan Likes, Founder of Bookkeeping Academy Online & Likes Accounting Company

About Meaghan:

Meaghan Likes superpower is taking people's fears out of their finances. She owns 5 businesses in Northern California…. her favorite of which is her window cleaning business (which she owns with her husband Jeff). And, while you wouldn't guess it from her personality, Meaghan's day "job" is working as a CPA. Meaghan's passion is educating and empowering other business owners across the world, by teaching them how to find financial freedom in their own lives. She is known as a disrupter in the accounting industry and her claim to fame is showing small business owners how to do their own bookkeeping correctly in less than 1 hour per month using Quickbooks Online. No accounting knowledge or experience is required. She teaches business owners smarter ways to make money, save money, and will inspire you to give back in meaningful ways. Meaghan helps thousands of home service business owners grow more profitable businesses through her training in Profits to Freedom. You can learn more about Meaghan and her products by visiting: profitstofreedom.com

JM: Hi Meaghan! Thank you so much for joining me around the campfire. I know you are a numbers guru and have a lot of great insight on business. Why is it so important for Home Service Providers to leverage data and build a budget to scale, not just go off their gut?

ML: I know this might sound crazy but it's actually quite easy to grow and scale a home service company these days. If you spend enough on marketing and advertising, you will make your phone ring, and as long as you answer it - you're likely to book the work and get paid.

The reason 75% of businesses fail in their first 15 years is not because making money is hard, they fail because they're bad at managing money. I know that as an accountant, I'm biased – I feel like the secret to a successful business is knowing your numbers.

Because growing the top line is not the problem... there are lots of people out there that can help you do that. It's having something to show for all your hard work when you're done paying your expenses at the end of every day, week, month and year... (that's the hard part!)

It's actually way more common for a company to grow their top-line revenue by a huge percentage and have their bottom-line revenue actually go backwards. Don't do that! Growing a bigger top line without a health profit margin is a bigger headache and a lot more stressful to run.

By knowing your numbers and paying attention to the bottom line (more than the top line) you're much more likely to be in the successful 25% of businesses that make it past their 15-year anniversary.

JM: You touched on some great points! Can you list the ranges in percentages where businesses should be to know if they are on the correct track on a monthly basis?

ML: The percentages I like to track are Cost of Goods Sold (COGS) and Net Profit Percentage. For COGS as a percentage of income, it will depend on your industry. For our window cleaning services, we look for no more than 45% in COGS, for gutter cleaning, we're more like 40%, if you do pressure washing/soft-washing, you can likely see as low as 35%.

If you don't know what your COGS as a percentage of your income is, ask your accountant/bookkeeper. If you aren't too crazy about your accountant/bookkeeper, touch base with me so I can support you at a higher level.

For tech pay – I like to say, be as generous as possible. A good starting exercise is to research the living wage in your state. That should be your minimum starting pay. And payroll should hang out between 25% and 40% of your gross receipts (depending on your industry. As an example, I live in California. And our living wage is $18.66/hour - if that is 30% of my gross revenue, then that means a technician should bill out at a minimum of $62.20/hour. If I want a 20% net profit percentage, that makes their labor rate $74.64. This means that in California - we can't afford to bill a technician (making barely a living wage) less than $75/hour. When you add in all of the employee benefits we offer, that number goes up by about 50%.

When you organize yourself to pay your people more - you then need to watch if your technicians are being efficient and confirm that they are actually getting the labor rate you budgeted for.

For target net profit percentages…. Historically, we've said 10-20% is considered healthy. If you're in growth mode – you'll have a lower net profit percentage. But if you keep an eye on your pricing and watch your profitability on a regular basis, you could see 20-30% net profit percentages consistently.

When we think about what percentage of income should be spent on advertising, it depends on what your goals are. If you're not profitable, I'd say keep it as close to 0 as possible. Once you're profitable, I think it depends on your phase of business. If you're in growth mode (and are already profitable), you could go as high as 15% advertising budget. Just keep a close eye on your metrics to make sure you're getting an ROI on your ad spend that's worth it. Where you're well-established with a strong brand, you'll likely drop back down to 5%

or less.

If percentages are scary to you, that's okay. They're actually quite hard to track, and the data can be difficult to rely on.

The first 5 numbers I recommend business owners start tracking when they want to improve their financial position are the following:

- Daily Gross Sales
- Average Ticket
- Conversion Rate
- Labor as a % of Income
- Net Profit Percentage

Choose one, start tracking it and watch it improve!

JM: This is pure gold. You've provided some valuable insights on the key percentages to track in order to improve your financial position as a business owner. Monitoring these numbers can definitely offer meaningful insights into the health and profitability of your business! As we progress, I wanted to make note of what a killer brand your window cleaning company has. I know you've recently rebranded the business. How did that impact the company and the growth overall?

ML: We rebranded with Dan Antonelli and his amazing team at KickCharge Creative. After nearly 14 years in business under a really old-school look, we were ready to update our image. We've aggressively raised our prices in recent years to be able to attract and retain good team members. To be able to afford to pay our employees more and offer generous benefits, we transferred those costs onto our customers in our pricing. The good news is that by taking better care of our employees we started to attract higher-quality candidates, they're happier and staying around longer. But after raising our prices so dramatically, our conversion rate took a bit of a hit. When the conversion rate dipped we realized there was a bit of a disconnect between our appearance and our pricing. The new branding finally brought alignment between the company we felt we were, a company people wanted to work for, and the company our clients see.

JM: It's fantastic to hear about how you came to the decision to rebrand. I love it. Something else I love is how much you serve and give back both inside and outside of your businesses. This leads me to my next question- Why should Service Companies put such an emphasis on giving back?

ML: When we first started our business, we did it for us. We wanted to stop punching a clock, and I wanted unlimited time off. We also hoped to make some money. Well, the making money part turned out to be pretty easy. Spending money, unfortunately, turned out to be even easier. From the beginning, I was a big budgeter and I practiced what I preached. Until we were making the income we wanted as owners and were profitable after paying ourselves that healthy income - I didn't invest anything in advertising and very little in marketing. But that doesn't mean we weren't marketing, we just got really good at guerrilla marketing. One of the first and quickest ways to do some marketing is to build a network, so we joined the chamber and both joined a service club. I'm a Rotarian, and my husband Jeff is a Kiwanian. We both spend about 10 hours a week giving back and enjoy giving away quite a bit of our net income each year. We find there's nothing that feels better than giving back to our community and giving back with both our time and our money. We stopped making money for us a long time ago, and we're too young to retire - although at less than 10 hours of work per week and 30 weeks off a year - I think we can agree that Jeff is semi-retired (before 40!). After my first trip to Africa, one of the partners I was working with on a project shook my hand as I left and looked me in the eyes and said, "go home and be successful, so that you can come back and help us." Talk about a WHY! Now we get up every day and work to make money for others. It has become part of our mission to be a generous place to work and to give back generously to our community. I have to say shifting our focus to making money for others has been so much more fun and rewarding!

JM: I really appreciate you sharing how your perspective has evolved over time. Making money proved to be relatively easy, but managing and spending it wisely posed its own challenges. By aligning your business with your values and giving back to your community, you have experienced fulfillment and made a positive impact. How does your business give back, and why did you choose this mission(s)?

ML: As a company, we started adding in volunteering last year. We started small by including our technicians in a toy drive. We took them out to a holiday breakfast, and instead of doing a white elephant, we took them shopping for a toy for kids living in poverty. They had so much fun on the shopping trip and then delivering their toys that we knew we had to build giving back into our company culture. My friend Martha Woodward has a program called Culture First, and we've learned so much in her program about getting to know our team and what motivates them. I think we're consistently seeing that millennials want more than a living wage and good benefits; they want to be a part of something bigger. We added 3 trucks to our fleet last year and when winter came... we had a really great team going but weren't quite at a full schedule. So we thought why not set up a fleet of volunteers on a weekly "meals on wheels" delivery route to keep them busy. It was such a success with our team that when spring hit, we decided to keep it going... Our teams now rotate weeks and we pay for every team member to volunteer a minimum of 2 hours per month serving meals to our financially fragile and home-bound seniors. There's no better feeling than being the only smile a senior might get in a day. And our team has really bonded by volunteering to help others each week. Upcoming volunteering opportunities with our company include planning a meal-filling kit event soon where we'll fill meal kits for families in developing countries. And adopting a federal holiday to hang flags downtown for Jeff's Kiwanis club. We have always preferred to spend our advertising budget either by rewarding our team for reviews or by giving to sponsor local nonprofit events. So we buy a table or two at one major fundraiser a quarter and invite our team and their significant others to join us out in the community and see first-hand who is benefitting from all of their hard work. Plus, there's some cool experiences for them, like Crab Feeds, Oktoberfest, Formal Dinners, BBQs and more! Giving back has become a part of our culture, and has really helped us get buy-in from our team to work towards our mission.

JM: It's truly inspiring to hear how your company has embraced the idea of giving back and incorporated volunteering into your company culture. Your leadership and dedication to giving back sets an exemplary standard for others to follow. One last question for you Meaghan before we leave the campfire, What advice do you have for anyone currently climbing their own mountain?

ML: Stick to YOUR "why" because I guarantee it's different than others.

I didn't break the 1-million-dollar mark in our home service company until 2022 (our 14th year in business). But I did it working less than 10 hours per month in my company (while building two other soon-to-be 7-figure businesses), and my husband worked less than 10 hours a week. All while traveling an average of 30 weeks per year (for work & fun).

We built a business slower than most (now you can get to 1 million with the help of some awesome coaching programs in 1-2 years), but we did it without ever sacrificing profitability, equity or family time.

Here are some examples of our non-negotiables.

It was important to us that Jeff stopped working nights and weekends in the first three years of our cleaning company, and he never went back. We don't want to be absentee owners, and we don't want to sell (for now).

What we do want is time and financial freedom to do what we want, when we want. So Jeff now works less than 10 hours a week, he can travel for many weeks on end without having to check in with anyone, and we pull off more than 25% as owner salaries plus still have double-digit profit margins.

So my advice is to stop looking at what everyone else is doing, stop coveting the online gurus, stop celebrating top-line revenues…

Think about why you started your company and focus on that. Build the company that you set out to build. Stay focused and true to that. Climb your own mountain, and before you know it you'll be ringing the bell!

TAKE ACTION:

1. Don't ever lose anything worthwhile if you can help it. How will you protect your mind and/business as life moves forward?
2. Post it on social media with the hashtags #protectthebell #ringthebell

CHAPTER 10:
A VIEW FROM THE TOP

Y ou put on your backpack and take one final look around before you head down. You notice that the sun is brighter, the air is cleaner, and your stress is gone. You have an overwhelming feeling of gratitude taking over. You look to the sky and thank God for the opportunity, and begin the wonderful descent back down. You see the crowds of people waiting to meet you. Some want to learn more about you. Others have burning questions such as who are you? What made you go up there? Who were you trying to get to notice you? What's with that flag tied to the bell?

That's when you smile with gratitude and experience one of the best feelings you will ever feel in life. That's when you realize that your initial mission is complete. Now it's time to go head back down the mountain so you can make a ton of money, help others and change the world.

🔔

Some people say it's lonely at the top. For me, it's a different type of answer because I feel like there's never truly an "I arrived" moment. I can, however, tell you that I have reached the highest peak that I've ever landed at, and it's somewhat freeing in many ways. This peak allows me to live the life of my dreams and also makes me feel like I'm maximizing my experience on this earth. But notice that I didn't say it's completely freeing? That's because it's not!

Long-term success is simply not guaranteed for anyone. There are so many important variables to making sure you metaphorically stay on top. When you make it to the top of a mountain, the view is beyond incredible. The feelings you have are unlike anything else you've ever experienced in your lifetime. That's exactly what the feeling is like when you make it to the top and ring the bell. The air is fresh, and you can breathe easily. The view is nothing short of miraculous.

There are also some bittersweet feelings because when you finally are able to breathe and take in your accomplishments, you can't help but remember all of the people that didn't believe in you and all of the moments that you wish you had more support. The sweet part is so much greater though. You really remember who was there for you during your most desperate and humble times. The view really helps you understand who truly cares about you and who would give you the shirt off their back to see you succeed in life. Simply put, the view from the top gives you clarity and a new, clearer perspective on life.

"When you make it to the top of a mountain, the view is beyond incredible. The feelings you have are unlike anything else you've ever experienced in your lifetime."

Jon Majak

The view wouldn't be amazing if we weren't able to talk about the money that comes with your success. For me, I literally came from a background where being poor was all I knew. I'll never forget the times my mom would hug me, crying when I was just a child and say: "we are poor son, we don't have much, but that's why I want you to dream big." But one of my favorite mantras that I tell myself often is that there are no real mistakes in life. In fact, I have found peace in knowing that my life was laid out far before I arrived. Napoleon Hill said it best: "Every adversity, every failure, every heartache carries with it the seed of an equal or greater benefit."

I believe my childhood and my early adulthood journey happened exactly like it was supposed to, full of good moments and also moments of pure struggle. I also believe this was my destiny to overcome all the odds and fulfill my greatest dreams. Not just for myself, but to be a force for good in life and show others that anything is possible if they want it bad enough.

Campfire Chat with Expert Climber:

Brandon Vaughn, Founder of Conquer

About Brandon:

Brandon scaled a very small service company with zero employees to over 60 and went from $8k/month to almost $500k/month in less than 6 seasons. He is passionate about creating a company culture where employees can thrive. He was awarded the 2017 S.B.A Small Business Person of the Year for the state of Oregon, and now helps small business owners "systemize" their companies.

JM: Hi Brandon, thank you so much for joining me around the campfire. It's such an honor to have you here, you've achieved so much, and your story is so inspiring. Let me ask, what does the view from the top look and feel like?

BV: Hi Jon, thank you for having me. Like many, I still feel like I'm on my journey and I can't wait to meet and be myself in two years. As I reflect back, I can tell you the things that motivate me the most or give me the most fulfillment are having the freedom to do what I want, when I want, with who I want at any point in time. I believe that reaching the top offers this type of freedom. I also find it extremely fulfilling to have the mental clarity to look back behind me and help others on their journey. It's the best feeling.

JM: Thanks so much for sharing that. It's inspiring to hear about this freedom and that you are helping others on their journey. You've beat so many odds and are changing this world, my friend. Let me ask, as you metaphorically gaze into the town below, what runs through your mind?

BV: I feel humbled and amazed. I think it's important to look back, celebrate the wins, intentionally take it all in and remember how far you've come. It's easy to get caught up in the day-to-day but just taking some time to pause and reflect is such an important part of the process.

JM: That's great advice. Reflection is a very vital part of the journey and if we don't look back down the mountain we will never realize how high we've actually climbed. Does your intuition tell you that you still have more mountains to climb and more peaks to reach?

BV: I feel like I have more impact to make and more personal growth to do. The one thing I will say is that the money side is the least fulfilling side of it. I know that money is a tool, and it has its benefits and is such a huge reward. It certainly has its place, but to me, time is the ultimate prize. Time is the ultimate currency. Money is infinite. You can make money, you can lose money, you can find money. You hear about entrepreneurs who lost it all and gained it all back and then some. The relationship with money is certainly infinite. There's infinite possibilities, infinite money. Look at Jeff Bezos, he can spend 9 million dollars an hour and never go down on his net worth, but yet he only has 20 or so years left to live. And every day, that time shrinks. For me, the ultimate definition of success and currency that I'm so appreciative of is precious time. I truly love spending time with family and those I love most. I can work from anywhere in the world with just a laptop. We can travel the world. We've been to Africa, Iceland and so many wonderful places.

JM: Thanks for sharing that, I think you hit on a really important point there. We really do only have a limited time on this earth and I think part of the climb is realizing that. Climbing up the mountain and making it to the top doesn't mean you will be satisfied with every single thing by any means. Considering you play at such a high-level, are you ever really satisfied?

BV: I think you have to force yourself to be satisfied sometimes. I believe the place where satisfaction comes from is from a place of gratitude, a place of humility, and a place of approaching where you are at with clarity. There are always ways to improve my mindset, my behaviors, and there's so many more people that I could help and serve and add value to. From that perspective, I'm uniquely wired to always be better than I was yesterday.

JM: I can totally relate to this and really appreciate your perspective here. What are the next levels for someone who wants to go further in their business?

BV: Depending on where the business owner is at, there are a lot of different directions they could take, whether it be franchising, licensing, or private equity, among many other routes. The most important lesson that I've learned is leveraging and thinking like an investor. For me, personally, I spend less than 20% of what I make on personal things. I'll then invest or save 80% of what my income is and roll it into other opportunities and investments. It's also safe to say that when your business gets to a place where you can truly get to be a semi-absentee owner, new challenges arise. I don't think anyone is fully absentee because you have to constantly and regularly be checking in with your CEO, General Managers and the people running those companies and holding them accountable. The goal is to always have more team members and systems in place so the business can function on its own. To me, I kind of view that as the next step for most business owners to take in their journey. This move allows themselves to be freed up to do whatever it is that fills their tank, whatever fulfills their "why", whether it's retire, traveling the world with their family, do ministry work, or whatever that looks like for them having more time to do what makes them truly happy is what it's all about.

JM: Such great insight Brandon, I really admire your outlook on everything. Thanks for spending some time around the campfire with me but before we get back to embarking on our journey's, I do have one last question to ask you. What's the best advice you can give to someone who is currently climbing their own mountain?

BV: The best advice I would give is to look up from time to time to cast what that view is going to look like when you get there but don't dwell there for too long because it can feel so far away. Remember, it's one step at a time. It's ok to look down and remember to consistently take one step day after day. When it comes to driving forward, pick a flag point or milestone that's not too far down the path. Focus on getting to that spot, then do it again and get to the next spot. The people who start at the bottom of the mountain and look all the way up there immediately start experiencing lots of negative self-talk. Something that sounds like: "that's too far. I'm never going to get there. I don't know if I have the ability, the agility, the stamina, or the endurance to make it." Instead, the secret is to keep your head down, be progressive, and charge forward one step at a time, and before you know it, inevitably, you will arrive. If every single day, you take one step, it's impossible not to arrive.

🔔

So when you get to the top of the mountain, and you have your arm around that bell, knowing you created the noise and made a lasting impact, you smile and realize that you are nothing like you were when you started your journey on the narrow road. I'm blessed to say that I have some money now. I'm able to live in the house of my dreams, support my family, put funds away for the future and am on track to retire when the time comes. Material things in life don't motivate me like they used to. Simply because I know when we leave this world, none of that is coming with me. I'm grateful for material things creating the spark within the younger version of me. These days, what truly matters to me is helping others and financial freedom. What matters to me is that my son never has to worry about finances in his life. What matters to me is that my wife can heal and grow without having the added financial stress she does not need. What matters to me is that I earned my seat at the table, and it was not given to me. I'm a big believer in doing things that make you feel good. And boy can I tell you, sitting on a high part of the mountain with intention and taking in the moment feels good. What most people don't tell you when they make it is that nothing is promised. There could be a catastrophic hurricane or tsunami that ruins your town or even demolishes the bell all to wash it away forever. So it's my job to keep on keeping on for as long as I can to make sure I don't get too comfortable. So it begs the question, how do you stay on top?

As I promised when I started this book, I will keep it straight-forward with you with zero fluff. My mountain, and yours, could come crumbling down right now. Certain variables you can't control, such as a recession, but other aspects come down to you and only you. Remember, everything lives and dies at the feet of the CEO, so if you don't protect your success with everything you've got and something bad happens, you only have one person to blame.

"Every adversity, every failure, every heartache carries with it the seed of an equal or greater benefit."

Napoleon Hill

Here's the strategy you must drive forward in order to always keep your success. I've nailed it down to 7 musts that need to be executed on.

First, enjoy your life. Be present in the good, bad, and indifferent moments. These are the moments that matter most, and if you are present in the moment, you will know if something feels off. If something feels off, it could be your intuition telling you to open your eyes and adjust your approach.

Second, take care of your health. When you have your health, you have everything. Do what is needed to care for your mind, body and soul, every single day.

Third, make your money work for you. Your money should be like little soldiers going out to capture and take more money. Invest in proven areas that drive returns, such as real estate, stocks and bonds, business and other areas where you see great potential. Keep a sharp eye out for innovations and where the future is headed, and always stay plugged into that.

Fourth, always have a coach or a mentor in your life. Turn them into life-long family members, and you will forever have a built-in business killer driving you to be the best version of yourself.

Fifth, make efforts to contribute your wisdom and coach or mentor others. Helping others break through is essential to your long-term success.

Sixth, educate yourself every single day through reading or positive audio. If you love to read, dive into books that will bring peace, purpose and profit in your life. If you are religious, I highly encourage you to open up scripture. If you are into listening, dive into inspirational podcasts and audiobooks. Doing this will enlighten you and help you in more ways than I can explain. Be determined to never stop learning.

Seventh, set life and business goals. Be detailed on where you want to be within the next 1,3,5, and 10 years. Then establish benchmarks to hit the measurable targets that will get you there.

When you are grinding through your narrow road and trudging up that mountain trying to pursue making money and making an impact, your life undoubtedly becomes extremely draining and exhausting at times. Take it from me, don't wait until you reach the bell to show up for yourself. Take care of yourself along the journey to the best of your ability. I found myself in some very dark places during the journey, and now that I have a clear perspective, I can tell you that when you arrive, your mental health restores super-fast. The mind and body are so resilient. You can refocus back on your spiritual health, vacations, and not being a slave to the business anymore. This is priceless. You always hear about when you don't have any struggles in life, you don't appreciate the little things. That's why it's good to embrace your struggle. Own it. Be proud of it because when you finally make it, life opens up so much.

So, my friend, it's been wonderful spending this time with you. Whether you've reached the top of the mountain by now or not, you should have massive clarity.

You should have a clear idea of how to make it through the narrow road and find a moment to gaze from the bottom and into the future.

You should be ready to charge up the highest mountain and smash the bell louder than you could ever imagine. You now know what it will look like when everyone in town can't help but look up at you in awe.

You are set up to make more money than ever and also create lasting impact for countless people. Henry David Thoreau once said: "It's not what you look at that matters, it's what you see."

As my final thoughts wind down, I want to say thank you for allowing me to be a part of your journey. Here's my hope for you. I hope you are now on track to make so much money that you need a team to help you manage it all. I hope you've intentionally made a difference in as many lives as possible. I hope when you look back down, you see how far you've actually come. Happy bell ringing!

TAKE ACTION:

1. Most business owners don't have a clear picture of what winning looks like? Is it selling your business? Is it starting a non-profit? Is it having an automated machine where everyone is making a ton of money and fosters a place where employees love what they do? What does success truly look like to you?
2. Write it out and post it on social media with the hashtags #viewfromthetop #ringthebell

If you've found value in this book, please take 60 seconds to write a quick review on Amazon.

As you know, this book was completely dedicated to helping you grow both personally and professionally. The greatest thing I can ask for in exchange for the value of the book is a review.

Gaining great reviews helps the algorithms showcase Ring the Bell over others. The more this book gets seen, the more impact it will deliver.

Thank you again.

Want some help growing your business?

Chat with Jon or a member of his team to learn how to grow your service business like never before!

Simply go to Grow.MrPipeline.com/Discovery